# The Body in the Text

## Interpretations

This series provides clearly written and up-to-date introductions to recent theories and critical practices in the humanities and social sciences.



In preparation:
Reconstructing theory, edited by David Roberts
After a fashion, by Joanne Finkelstein
Hypertext, by Ilana Snyder
German feminist theory, by Silke Beinssen-Hesse
and Catherine Rigby

# The Body in the Text

Anne Cranny-Francis

MELBOURNE UNIVERSITY PRESS
1995

Melbourne University Press
PO Box 278, Carlton South, Victoria 3053, Australia

First published 1995



Designed by Mark Davis/text-art
Typeset by Melbourne University Press in 10.5/13 pt Garamond
Printed in Malaysia by SRM Production Services Sdn Bhd

ISSN 1039-6128

National Library of Australia Cataloguing-in-Publication entry

Cranny-Francis, Anne
The body in the text.
Bibliography.
Includes index.
ISBN 0 522 84575 4.
1. Body image. 2. Body, Human—Social aspects. 3. Body, Human—Symbolic aspects. I. Title. (Series: Interpretations).

306.4

*For Jim, Hamish and Conal*

# Contents

Preface ........................................................ *ix*

1 Introduction: Written on the Body .................... *1*

Mind/body dualism .................................................. *3*

Feminist critiques .................................................. *4*

Theorists of class and race ...................................... *7*

The 'normal' body .................................................. *8*

From consciousness to embodied subjectivity ................ *10*

Postmodern bodies .................................................. *12*

Bodies and technology: cyborg bodies ........................ *15*

Postmodern bodies and desire .................................. *16*

Foucault ................................................................ *18*

2 (En)acting, (Per)forming Gender: Bodies, Sexes, Sexualities ........................................ *22*

Politicising the gendered body .................................. *23*

(En)acting gender: bodies, sexes, sexualities ................ *27*

(Re)production: gender in performance ........................ *33*

3 Embodying the Other: Inscriptions of Race and Ethnicity ........ 44
Racial stereotyping and bodily inscription ........ 46
Bodies and ethnicities ........ 59
Race and ethnicity: degrees of 'otherness' ........ 63

4 Classifying Bodies: Inscriptions of Class ........ 66
Class(ify)ing the body ........ 67
Sexuality: class and/of the body ........ 70
Body techniques: classing the body ........ 77

5 Cyborgs and Wet-ware: Technologised Bodies ... 88
Cyborgs: machine-men and the man-made body ........ 89
Cyborg manifesto: (re)positioning the cyborg ........ 98
Wet-ware: infotech and embodiment ........ 99
Rhizome versus gap: new conceptualisations of desire .... 102

6 Conclusion: The Body in the Text ........ 106
The body and/as the text ........ 107
Embodying new femininities and masculinities ........ 109
The body in the text ........ 112

Bibliography ........ 114

Index ........ 124

# Preface

It occurred to me only in hindsight that *The Body in the Text* seems like nothing so much as the title of a detective novel, or at least a critical exploration of detective novels as a genre. In working through the many different theoretical and critical writings on the body I often felt like a detective, looking for the issues and concerns which would provide the clue to what seems a relatively recent fascination with 'the body'. 'Seems' may be a crucial term here, since one of the interesting things I learned from this study is that the cultures of all times and places have always been vitally concerned with 'the body', whether that means the artful delineation of bodies and embodied practices in indigenous Australian paintings, the narratives of everyday life in the tombs of Egyptian pharaohs, the battles of Renaissance painters to produce a new understanding of human embodiment against the theological certainties of the Catholic church, or the embodied rebellions of Luddites in the late eighteenth and early nineteenth centuries as they smashed the machinery which was to change forever their way of life and perceptions of the body. Yet recently western societies seem to be undergoing another renaissance of interest in notions of embodiment, which coincides with enormous changes in their social, political and economic composition, as well as in the technology that typically characterises them. These, then, were my sources or clues for an exploration of the many ways in which notions of embodiment—the bodily inscription of material and discursive change—have been interrogated in recent texts.

Those I analyse here include both theoretical studies and fictional texts—literary, film, televisual and others. The reason for the particularity of my title, *The Body in the Text,* is that I want to explore not only the abstract, conceptual arguments that constitute one part of the current debate on 'the body', but also some of those texts (particularly popular texts) in which this debate appears as a figure, a problematic, a fictional expression or a combination of these. In some chapters the work of particular theorists is treated in some detail, since their contribution to the debate is especially important and stimulating; for example, Judith Butler in Chapter 2, Homi Bhabha in Chapter 3, and Lynette Finch and Marcel Mauss in Chapter 4. In Chapter 5, however, the most interesting contribution comes from a fictional text, James Cameron's film, *Terminator 2: Judgement Day.* All of these different kinds of text participate in those (re)conceptualisations of the body which in the west are currently challenging traditional values and understandings of embodiment. They both act on and enact the discursive practices that inscribe late twentieth-century bodies.

In her novel, *Written on the Body* (1993), Jeanette Winterson observes:

> Written on the body is a secret code only visible in certain lights: the accumulations of a lifetime gather there. In places the palimpsest is so heavily worked that the letters feel like braille. I like to keep my body rolled up away from prying eyes. Never unfold too much, tell the whole story. I didn't know that Louise would have reading hands. She has translated me into her own book. (Winterson, 1993: 89)

Late twentieth-century western (re)readings of the body constitute a 'translation' that is simultaneously an analysis and a critique of both the material and discursive practices in which the body is implicated, and by which it is controlled and regulated. Furthermore, this translation is often utopian, working to open up (by a judicious word here, a phrase there) new possibilities arising from the translator's detection of contradictions and anomalies in the practices inscribing those bodies. These will become the grounds for (re)conceptualisations of the corporeal, and for the production of new and different bodies not limited by the regulatory practices of the past.

> This is where the story starts, in this threadbare room. The walls are exploding. The windows have turned into telescopes. Moon and stars are magnified in this room. The sun hangs over the mantelpiece. I stretch out my hand and reach the corners of the world. The world is bundled up in this room. Beyond the door, where the river is, where the roads are, we shall be. We can take the world with us when we go and sling the sun under your arm. Hurry now, it's getting late. I don't know if this is a happy ending but here we are let loose in open fields. (Winterson, 1993:190)

1

# Introduction: Written on the Body

The first and perhaps most fundamental move in the reassessment of the body was the critique of one of those many dualisms which have structured western thought—the mind/body dualism. This critique has been a feature of politicised writings by feminists as well as by theorists of class and race. Each questions the way in which the mind/body dualism—displaced on to dualisms of gender (masculine/feminine), class (middle-class/non middle-class) and race (Anglo/non-Anglo)—reproduces the inequitable valuation of its constituent terms, and results in a powerfully discriminatory conception of the 'normal' body which ensures the cultural dominance of such positionings as 'masculine', 'Anglo', and 'middle-class'.

This dualism has been considered also through a reconceptualisation of the place of the individual in society. For most of the twentieth century the individual has been theorised both politically and psychoanalytically in terms of consciousness. This focus on consciousness has reinforced the positive valuation of 'mind' and (by omission) negative valuation of 'body'. More recent theorists, however, have replaced this notion of consciousness with a conceptualisation of the individual that includes experiences of society, and notably resistance to and compliance with those networks of discourses and material practices that constitute the everyday real. Inevitably these are embodied experiences. The individual who reflects on them is conceptualised therefore as an embodied subjectivity, part of and inscribed by the discursive and material practices of society. So the exploration of both individual experience and the nature of not only subjectivity but also contemporary social practice has come to include an analysis of body inscription.

Yet another critical perspective on the body has been contributed by postmodernist writers, many of whom critique the duality between reality and representations of it. In the age of the simulacrum, of the model with no 'real life' referent, this dualism is particularly perverse. One focus of postmodern interrogation has been the 'representation' of woman, and how 'real' female bodies are inscribed by those 'representations'. And the same kind of analysis has been applied not only to masculine bodies but also to the bodies of other sexualities, races, ethnicities, ages and classes. In other words, postmodern critics also conceptualise the material body as inscribed by those discourses and material practices that constitute its social environment.

To push such analyses a step further involves re-examining the nature of that environment, the everyday real of a society with a rapidly changing technology. Working from the premise that bodies are socially constituted in and by material and discursive practices—and given that those practices are changing—it follows that bodies, too, are changing. The contemporary (western) body is the product of an information technology society, the so-called 'cyborg' body whose name conflates the '*cyb*ernetic' (the study of systems of control and communication within animals and machines) with the '*org*anic'. Much recent writing on the body is concerned with analysing the nature, limits and modes of existence of this cyborg body. When the familiar and dualised modernist body is replaced with the postmodern cyborg body then our conceptualisation of desire must also change. The 'deficit' model of desire, in which desire is produced by some kind of lack or gap between the desiring subject and the desired object, is simply inadequate for a wired-in, networked, and intertextual body. Instead, desire comes to be conceptualised as a productive mechanism, a continual process of stimulation, connection and (re)production. Such a mechanism is theorised most thoroughly in the work of Michel Foucault, who focused critical attention on the ways in which not only the mind but also the body is subject(ed) to those material and discursive conditions and imperatives in which the social subject lives. (These matters are discussed briefly at the end of this chapter.)

This chapter traces the contexts within which contemporary readings of and writings on 'the body' are being performed. They derive from two different but complementary perspectives: from overtly politicised analyses performed by theorists of gender, sexuality, class, race, ethnicity and age; and from postmodernist critics whose challenges are also fundamentally political, but which focus primarily on the body in a state of change, the cyborg body. They begin by interrogating the basic dualism in which the body is implicated—the mind/body dualism.

## Mind/body dualism

Since the foundational philosophy of the Greeks, western thinking has constructed the mind and the body as opposite to one another. The effects of this dualism can be seen only when we consider how it is valorised. As the work of Jacques Derrida and others has illustrated, such dualisms generally operate by constructing one term as the negative of (but necessary precondition for) the other. In western philosophical discourse, 'body' has been constructed traditionally as the negative other of 'mind', though it is nevertheless the condition of existence for the category of 'mind'.

The consequences of this negative valorisation of 'body' are far-reaching. In an article on *anorexia nervosa* Susan Bordo (1988) summarises these consequences. First, she notes that 'the body is experienced as alien, as the not-self, the not-me'. This results in the instrumentalisation of the body as crude matter at the command of the will or intellect. There is no integrity of *being* under such a regime, which opens the way for uses to be made of the body from which the mind is divorced, or which the mind cynically controls. Bodily activity can thus be dismissed as essentially alien to the mind, wherein lies the true essence of self. The social and political implications of this attitude hardly need amplification, but I shall return to this point later.

Bordo observes that another consequence of this dualism is that 'the body is experienced as *confinement* and *limitation*: a 'prison', a 'swamp', a 'cage', a 'fog'. . . This follows from the previous point, of course. If the mind is the pure essence of self, the body can be perceived only as an unnecessary, confining, even polluting presence. The metaphors Bordo cites are crucial here: as a 'prison' or 'cage', the body traps the essential mind; like a 'swamp' it pollutes that purity of essence; and it confuses the real, pure, essential self by the 'fog' of its physical imperatives. These metaphors are as negative as the primary apperceptions discussed.

Related to this is the notion of the body as the *enemy*. This is seen very clearly in the Christian theology which is based on that earlier Greek philosophy. In the writings of St Augustine the body is presented unequivocally as the deadly enemy of the mind, will, spirituality and intellect. The body holds us back from spiritual apotheosis; it is torn by physical temptations which must be resisted if the pure self is to ascend to another, higher (than bodily) state. The body must therefore be disciplined, controlled and used as the mind requires to achieve this end. Hence Bordo's final point is that 'the body is the locus of all that threatens our attempts at *control*. It overtakes, it overwhelms, it erupts and disrupts' (Bordo, 1988:92). She again quotes Augustine's imprecations against the body, as the site of 'slimy desires of the flesh', noting that 'Plato, Augustine, and, most explicitly, Descartes provide instructions, rules, or models of how to gain control over the body, with the ultimate aim of learning to live without it' (ibid.:93).

Although this latter aim may seem a bit self-defeating, it is a desire often expressed by those who were the focus of Bordo's research, namely people suffering *anorexia nervosa*. Yet it is not simply those suffering some form of physical pathology who express this disdain for the body. Rather it seems that anorexics make explicit the mind/body dualism of much western and Christian thought.

## Feminist critiques

Feminists began to consider the mind/body duality quite explicitly in the 1970s. Writing in 1978 about the development of patriarchal subjectivity, Eva Figes noted:

> If mind becomes the motor force of matter, it nevertheless implies a split, whereupon mind is extolled at the expense of matter. Just as earlier Christians distinguished between body and soul, and tended to portray woman as the incarnation of physical lust, the idealists also tended to make an evaluative split between mind and physical matter, with mind as male and the body, loathsome and sordid, as female. (Figes, 1978:122)

When we recognise how the negative term in mind/body dualism is conflated with other concepts such as femininity, then its social and political significance is even more striking. The French feminist writer Hélène Cixous traces the use of this metaphor in her introduction to *Sorties* (1981):

> *Where is she?*
>
> Activity/passivity,
> Sun/Moon,
> Culture/Nature,
> Day/Night,
>
> Father/Mother,
> Head/heart,
> Intelligible/sensitive,
> Logos/Pathos.
>
> Form, convex, step, advance, seed, progress.
> Matter, concave, ground—which supports the step, receptacle.
> Man
> ———
> Woman
>
> Always the same metaphor: we follow it, it transports us, in all of its forms, wherever a discourse is organized. The same thread, or double tress leads us, whether we are reading or speaking, through literature, philosophy, criticism, centuries of representation, of reflection. (Cixous, 1981:90)

Cixous traces a history of what she terms the '*hierarchized* oppositions' (ibid.:91) by which woman is constituted in western thinking. One of these is the mind/body dualism as realised in her list of formulations which follow the Father/Mother dyad or couple. By her implication in this series, Woman is defined and described as the negative 'other' of Man, while at the same time being the necessary term for his existence; that is, Man is the primary and positive term of this dualism only as long as Woman remains the negative and secondary term. This implicit denigration of Woman can be traced in social practices that systematically devalue and marginalise the role of women.

When feminists asserted in the early 1970s that 'the personal is political' they were not merely asking for a more equitable home life. They were rejecting a public/private dualism (with its familiar hierarchisation) which was often used to justify the maintenance of inequalities between men and women. At the same time they argued that it was not a dualism at all, because the division is neither valid nor actual. The behaviours, values and attitudes that characterise the public sphere can also be seen at work in the private sphere—and nowhere more so than in the behaviour of those who campaign publicly for equality, but privately enact a wholly different set of practices (a distinction which is the experience of many women). This dualism is destroyed by demonstrations that its terms are identical. So too is the traditional dualism of mind/body, whose social and political consequences are manifest in the Man/Woman dyad and its constitutive metaphors. This is not simply to say that Man equals Woman, but that each term is produced in its traditional sense (and with traditional consequences) by one particular philosophical or metaphysical move, namely the mind/body dualism. In other words, by asserting that 'the personal is political', feminist writers subvert or disrupt one of the fundamental dualisms that structures western thought.

The motivation for feminist writers to engage in this kind of philosophical or discursive exercise is to change the social practices engendered by these '*hierarchized* oppositions'. For Cixous, an engagement with the constitutive metaphors of western culture is not a game of semantics but a discursive intervention aimed at producing material changes: in the ways women are not only perceived and treated, but also perceive and treat themselves. For feminist writers, to challenge the mind/body dualism was and remains a political act. Chapter 2 deals at greater length with the body politics of feminism, particularly in its more recent manifestations. However, it is important at this stage to note that feminist writings of the 1960s and 1970s engaged with the significances of western perceptions and valorisations of the 'body' in ways that helped prepare the grounds for a more rigorous analysis of its discursive construction.

## Theorists of class and race

During the 1960s and 1970s cultural critics engaged in the politics of class and race increasingly observed that the conventions by which working-class and non-Anglo people were constructed were in terms that aligned them with animality, physicality and the body, rather than with civilisation, humanity and the mind. Here the same set of metaphors can be seen in action. And again it is the devaluing of the body (in the mind/body dualism) that maintains the supremacy of the 'mind' component and those social attributes or positionings—such as Anglo, middle-class—it is used to construct. In *Learning to Labour* (1980) for example, Paul Willis describes the revalorisation by young working-class men of the 'mental/manual' dualism which was used to grade them educationally (Willis, 1980:148). By giving high value to the 'manual' term, these young men were able in the short term to construct for themselves a prestige and status denied them within the broader social context. Unfortunately, because that revalorisation does not extend beyond the class in which it originates, it operates simultaneously as a way of maintaining them in the disempowered position to which they are assigned socially. These young men can reverse but not challenge the terms of that dualism, which can be reasserted by a conventional valorisation in another context.

The politics of race were being contested even more actively in the west. In the United States, Martin Luther King, Malcolm X and many others bodily confronted the inequities that defined their existence within that society. Their political activism and revolutionary rhetorics (despite individual differences between figures such as King and Malcolm X) effected a refusal of the dualisms that circumscribed their lives. Perhaps this is one of the reasons why King's 'I Have a Dream' speech is so powerful: his opening move is an appropriation of the intellectual and imaginative voice so long denied black men and women in the United States (and indigenous and other non-Anglo peoples in countries such as Australia).

Chapters 3 and 4 consider more closely the bodily articulations of class and race. Here again the analyses by cultural critics of the constitution of identities of class and race refer ultimately to that structuring dualism of mind/body which they consistently attempt to disrupt or subvert. Such activities in turn disrupt or subvert the significations associated with that dualism, and which are incorporated into the social constitution of specific subjectivities.

The context in which to place the development of and interest in the discursive construction of the body is therefore in part the political activism and theoretical writing (those terms are not to be read as a dualism) of feminists, anti-classist and black activists in the 1960s and 1970s. In one sense, it is the next step in their analysis of the constitution of particular kinds of subjectivities.

## The 'normal' body

One of the earliest engagements with the notion of how the body is constructed materially and discursively came through the deconstruction of what constitutes the 'normal' body. Cultural theorists such as Foucault, Cixous and Willis treat 'the body' as a term in a dualism that operates strategically to devalue a whole range of social and cultural positionings. In another set of significations, however, it is used to define what is normal and therefore valued and valid. Feminist critics, for example, have pointed to the many ways in which assumptions about the 'normal' body define it as male. This assumption is seen in a wide range of social practices and material goods, from the design of furniture to the provision of sick leave and maternity leave. A 'normal' body does not need maternity leave because 'normal' bodies (being male) do not get pregnant. In fact, even with the best of intentions in some cases, pregnancy and other distinctly feminine bodily states have to be pathologised as illnesses so that women can be granted the provisions they need in order to continue in their employment while also having families.

Similar assumptions can be found across a whole range of social and discursive positionings. The 'normal' body tends to be not only male, but also middle-class, from an Anglo cultural background, heterosexual, and aged somewhere between twenty-five and forty. Of course, this body is and was never numerically dominant. It is, however, the body which people imagine when they think of the 'average person' or 'average joe [*sic*]'. It is also the body for which chairs and buses were designed and counter tops built, and which is the recipient of social security and employment benefits of various kinds. This is the body that corresponds to the so-called generic 'man', the use of the masculine pronoun to encompass all genders and sexualities. Yet as Dale Spender (quoted in Hekman, 1990:33) remarks so acutely, the notion that 'man has difficulty in childbirth' does not make much sense. The assumption that there is a normal body does not make a great deal of sense either, although it is surprisingly persistent in discursive constructions and material practices. The 'normal' body is not just an inaccurate generalisation which disadvantages a lot of people. It is also a technology for maintaining the social dominance of a particular discursive positioning: Anglo, middle class, masculine, heterosexual and youthful to middle aged.

To take an extreme instance, the recently abandoned practice in South Africa of determining each person's social status by a measure which depended in part on the relative whiteness of their skin and curliness of their hair is most obviously an oppressive practice—particularly in a society in which the characteristics most damned (black skin, tightly curled hair) characterise by far the greatest number of inhabitants. The same practices were used to admit or bar African Americans from night clubs earlier this century. Indigenous Australians, too, were judged by identical criteria when they were forcefully removed from their parents and taken to boarding schools; if their skin colour was pale, these children would be separated from their own people and raised as foster children in white families, where they were encouraged to forget their own cultural heritage. In these instances the 'normal' body is pale-skinned with straight hair, and the consequences of not having that body can be devastating, since the only options are either total marginalisation or an acceptance dependent on the individual's rejection of her or his cultural inheritance.

I shall return to this notion of the 'normal' body. I raise it here as part of the context in which critical and theoretical interest in 'the body' has come to supersede the former focus on ideology or subjectivity or consciousness.

## From consciousness to embodied subjectivity

From the mid-nineteenth to the mid-twentieth centuries, critical analyses of the positioning of individuals within society (and of the power relations in which they are implicated) focused on the systems by which such power relations operated. Every individual was assumed to enact her or his positioning within the system relatively unproblematically. The most extreme statement of this conception of the individual is a reductive reading of Louis Althusser's essay on 'Ideology and Ideological State Apparatuses' (1971), in which the notion of the individual being 'interpellated' or called forth by ideology in order to take up a particular position in society becomes a kind of determinism. Individuals are believed to be incapable of resisting such ideological positioning. Moreover, they cannot even conceive the possibility of resistance, unless perhaps they happen to be social theorists who write essays like Althusser's.

In 'real life', however, people resist their ideological positionings, although they are inconsistent in the various ways in which they both resist and enact those positionings. The theoretical pressure to explain these apparent inconsistencies has given prominence to psychoanalytic discourses, primarily Freudian and post-Freudian discourses (such as the work of Jacques Lacan and Julia Kristeva). One line of (psychoanalytically inspired) thought suggests that the reasons for these inconsistencies and disjunctions can be located in the pathology of the individual. The problem with this approach is that it asserts the primacy of the system (as analysts perceive it) over the lived experience of the individual subject. Recent feminist critiques of Freud demonstrate that he was unable to accept descriptions by his female patients of their own experiences. Instead Freud pathologised those women as hysterics, and attempted to induce them to renounce their understanding of their experiences in favour of his authoritative (phallocentric) interpretations. The basic premise of their treatment was that they should be prepared to have their experience so radically recontextualised that their own bodily (hysterical) response would be shown to be simply the result of a misunderstanding.

In rejecting this Freudian procedure, critics of psychoanalysis have argued instead that individual responses need to be understood within the network of social relationships in which a particular person is involved. They reject that model of individual practice that is based on the notion of a consciousness more or less suitably constituted for life within a particular social context. Instead they perceive subjectivity as formed within the network of material and discursive practices that constitute the individual's experience.

One such critique comes from psychoanalyst and Freudian commentator Lacan, who specifically situates the formation of subjectivity within those discursive practices that constitute the individual's early environment. However, Lacan conceptualises those practices from within an essentially Freudian and phallocentric model, which he sees as structuring the subjectivity of each individual. Again, such a model gives the individual little opportunity to resist this 'interpellation', despite the fact that resistances apparently take place. And again the individual's lived experience seems to have little if any place in the theory. Of course, this Lacanian model of the formation of subjectivity can be (and has been) modified in ways which make it useful for theorists who do indeed value the material and bodily experiences of the individual subject. An example is the work of Catherine Belsey, who argues that the theories of both Althusser and Lacan can be modified by accepting that each individual encounters not just one ideology but rather an enormous complexity of discourses. These discourses are negotiated in a specific way by each of us as a result of our particular experiences and positionings, which are conventionally described in terms of variables such as gender, class, race, ethnicity, sexuality and age. In other words, Belsey's conceptualisation of individual subjectivity makes a place for the individual's experience of the world in terms of emotional, intellectual, spiritual and bodily apprehensions of it. Accordingly, each individual subject is constituted through those complex negotiations.

Psychoanalytic theorists such as Kaja Silverman, Jane Gallop and Luce Irigaray have also reassessed the work of both Freud and Lacan. They, too, in different ways, have reconstructed psychoanalytic discourse in order to produce an embodied subject rather than a more or less traumatised (phallocentric) consciousness. In each case a key analytic move is to compare the lived experiences of psychoanalytic subjects with the conclusions one would reach by following Freudian or Lacanian models or both. The work of these theorists will be discussed at greater length in Chapter 2. I simply note here that the critique of psychoanalysis has come not only from other disciplines (as in the case of Foucault and Belsey) but also from within psychoanalysis itself. And it has focused on the extent to which psychoanalytic discourse has tended to ignore or repress the body of the subject in order to produce a disembodied consciousness which might then be modified in chosen ways. Critics of Freud and Lacan have posited instead a material subject, whose embodied subjectivity results from a complex negotiation of those discursive and material practices in which it is enmeshed.

From yet another perspective, then, the ground is being prepared for a reassessment of how the body is perceived. This deals with such matters as its crucial role in the production of the individual subject, who both is and is of that body; the ways in which bodies are marked or tattooed by individual experiences of the world; and how such body-markings contribute to subsequent experiences, and hence to the (re)negotiation of individual subjectivities as embodied subjects.

## Postmodern bodies

'The body' is also the subject of postmodernist concerns with issues of ontology (the essence of things or being in the abstract) and epistemology (theory of knowledge). What is the body? How are its limits defined? What space or place does it occupy? In a social context which is becoming increasingly information-based, how should the modernist (instrumental) conception of the body be rethought? How is this body 'known'? What is the relationship between the material body and its discursive constructions?

Many postmodernist analyses deal with the relationship between the 'real' and 'representation'. This used to be an unproblematic duality, like mind/body: the body was the real material fact, and representation was a reflection of it. Then the reflection began to construct the real. As Cindy Sherman demonstrates in her photographs, people construct their 'real' bodies in the image of those images of bodies they see at the movies and in the media: Sherman photographs herself in settings and costumes which are either copied from old movies, or look as if they are (Owens, 1983). Again the postmodernist response is not a simple inversion—elevating 'representation' at the expense of the 'real'—but a demonstration of how the category of the 'real' is dependent on the notion of 'representation'. Elizabeth Grosz describes this deconstructive reading practice in this way:

> Derrida's [deconstructive] reading strategies involve *both* reversal and displacement together: the dichotomy must be reversed (showing that the terms are not logically necessary or unalterable in their hierarchical relation); and the repressed must be displaced, not *out of the structure altogether* but by positioning it within the core of the dominant term, as its *logical condition*. (Grosz, 1989:30)

Sherman's work is classically Derridean. It locates the constructed image as the condition of existence of those real, material bodies we see around us. It does so not to assert the primacy or dominance of those representations, but to show the intertextual network of discursive and material practices in which all of us are both implicated and constituted, bodily and otherwise.

Many other postmodern artists work in a similar way, demonstrating the inscription of the material and the discursive on the embodied subject. Madonna's 'Material Girl' video is a popularisation of the same theme. There Madonna inscribes herself as Marilyn Monroe, in a move which demonstrates not only the power of the image (Monroe) but also the dependence of our understandings of the 'real' (woman) on contemporary 'representation'. After all, who is the 'star' of this video, Madonna or Monroe? And what readings (deconstructive or phallocentric or both) does it construct? Madonna subsequently made this image-play the focus of her career with interesting and complex results, as revealed by contributors to the collection, *Madonnarama* (Frank and Smith, 1993).

Sherman and Madonna are particularly concerned with the production of the female body. Indeed, postmodernist interrogations of 'the body' have tended to focus on women's bodies. In one sense this phenomenon reproduces the mind/body dualism discussed earlier, with 'body' being read as metaphorically synonymous with 'woman'. There are other reasons, however, for this focus on the production of the female body, not the least being the consistent use of the female body as an 'object of desire' in a wide range of discourses and texts ('representations'). For critics intent on challenging the positioning of women in those networks of discourses and material practices that constitute contemporary social life, an important political move has been to critique these 'representations' of 'woman'. What we can now see also in such interrogations, however, is an assessment of the production and inscription of the 'body' in and by contemporary material and discursive practices.

Similar assessments are now being made of male bodies—in fact, of bodies of all kinds of sexualities, ethnicities, ages and social classes. The interest in male bodies is evident in different kinds of texts, ranging from advertising through movies to critical essays. There has been a marked increase in the use of male bodies in advertising strategies which seem to mirror the use of women's bodies, that is, as objects of desire. This has prompted critical responses which range from questions about the function of what appears to be role-reversal to the nature of the target audiences for such advertising. In turn this raises the question of how audiences are positioned by such texts, as well as about the ways in which consumers incorporate these images into their everyday lives. Some analyses of the production of male bodies deal not with 'marked' texts (like advertising images and their construction of particular styles and aesthetics) but with other everyday techniques for the production of male bodies, for example, in sport.

## Bodies and technology: cyborg bodies

Other reconceptualisations of the male body focus more on its instrumentalisation in the context of contemporary information technologies. Obvious examples are cyborg characters such as Leon and Roy Batty in *Blade Runner* (Ridley Scott, 1982), the terminators in *The Terminator* (James Cameron, 1984) and *Terminator 2: Judgment Day* (James Cameron, 1990), and Ripley's cyborg colleague in the *Alien* movies (Ridley Scott, 1979; James Cameron, 1986; David Fincher, 1992). In a sense, these characterisations do not move beyond the conventional, which tends to equate the male body with technology and instrumentality and the female body with nature and receptivity. In this respect they may be seen as simply updated versions of familiar dualisms. In another sense, however, the overdetermined technophilia of their construction begs certain questions. So too does their gender stereotyping: female cyborgs always tend to be 'pleasure models' (*Blade Runner*), whereas male cyborgs are either 'combat models' (*Blade Runner*) or unskilled manual labourers. What kind of new masculinity (and femininity) is being produced here? Surely it must not be coincidental that the most recognisable contemporary cyborg is enacted and embodied by an actor whose own body is already a virtual caricature of stereotypical masculinity, the ex-Mr Universe, Arnold Schwarzenegger. The contrast between Schwarzenegger and television's most famous android—Data of *Star Trek: The Next Generation* (1988–94), played and embodied by the slim actor and mime artist, Brent Spiner—makes the choice of actor even more marked. The *Terminator* movies, like *Blade Runner*, attract an interest that seems to go beyond their accomplished story-telling and technological craft. Perhaps it is because they capture contemporary anxieties about both masculinity (and femininity) and the body in a time of rapid technological change.

This revolutionary development of information technologies of unprecedented power and scope challenges us to define even the limits of the body. Or, perhaps more correctly, it makes us re-examine the assumption that the body is easily delimited. If, for example, we try to define the body as the material (flesh and blood) part of our subjectivity, then how do we deal with prosthetic devices such as false teeth, cochlear implants and coronary pacemakers? If we are prepared to bend our definition of the material body to include these devices, then how do we deal with virtual-reality devices which displace it into cyberspace? That is, do we need to place limits on the extensions of the body's sensory capacities beyond what we conventionally think of as 'real' or material (i.e. what we can see, hear, touch, smell, taste)? If we relax those limitations, then how do we deal with the extension of the body over electronic networks that now span the globe? Is the body simply the 'wet-ware' which sits in front of the keyboard gazing at the computer screen, or does the wet-ware–PC interface produce a new, composite, cyborg body? These questions will be examined further in chapters 5 and 6. It is clear, however, that our ontological understanding of the body is under serious reconsideration in the closing decades of the twentieth century, and that this is related to developments in those technologies that, to some extent, define the kind of society in which we live and the individual relationships (both interpersonal and institutional) that constitute it.

## Postmodern bodies and desire

The concept which dominated theoretical discourse—and book covers—before it was displaced by 'the body' is 'desire'. Obviously, one might think, the two are related. That is an assumption, however, which must also be placed in the context of changes in the conceptualising of the body. The notion of desire which has dominated thinking for most of the twentieth century is fundamentally Freudian, and treats desire as a response to a perceived lack. This metaphor is used and amplified in Lacan's psychoanalytic theory, as explained by Grosz: 'It is the movement from one signifier to another, which Lacan claims is the very movement of *desire,* the endless substitution of one object of desire for another, none of which is adequate to fill the original lack propelling desire—the lost or renounced mother' (Grosz, 1989:24). This notion of desire as 'negative, a hole, an unfillable absence' (ibid.:xvi) is located, as Grosz notes, within a tradition which extends from Plato through Hegel and Lacan to the work of contemporary theorists such as

Kristeva. It is also a metaphor particularly suited to the conceptualisation of 'body' as the negative other of 'mind'.

Like the mind/body dualism, the notion of desire as lack (re)produces the conception of mind as separate from body, and constitutes the body as the material ground on which desire is experienced (whether that desire be primarily physical, emotional, intellectual, or spiritual). Desire is produced in the transformation of bodily affects (feelings or responses) into mental or intellectual processes which may be more or less conscious or deliberate. Such bodily affects are assumed to be subservient to the controlling mind, which ensures the continual displacement of the object of desire so that satisfaction is never achieved. In Lacanian terms, desire is a state of endless displacement.

When the traditional relationship between mind and body is challenged, so too is the conception of desire. Once the mind/body dualism is replaced by a conception of embodied subjectivity (in which 'body' becomes the grounds for existence of the category 'mind'), then it makes no sense to think of desire as a lack affectively realised (in physiological responses and feelings) and mentally transformed. There is simply no separation, no space of lack, to be filled. Instead we need a concept of desire that replicates the situation of the embodied subject within a network of material and discursive practices. For such an embodied subject, desire is 'not a lack but a positive force of production. It is no longer identified with a purely psychical and signifying relation, but is a force or energy which creates links between objects, which makes things, forges alliances, produces connections' (ibid.:xvi). As Grosz goes on to note (paraphrasing Gilles Deleuze and Félix Guattari in *Anti-Oedipus*), this concept of desire is not primarily mental or psychical as Lacan's is, but 'permeates all modes of production, and all linkages, psychical, social, mechanical' (ibid.:xvi).

The metaphor which best expresses the complexity and interconnectedness of this notion of desire is Deleuze and Guattari's 'rhizome'. Taken from botany (a stem that can produce both roots and shoots, from the Greek *rhiza*, 'root'), it images the interlocking, enmeshed web of discourses and practices in which the subject is (re)produced. Rejecting the simplistic notion of dualisms, Deleuze and Guattari write:

> There is a rupture in the rhizome each time the segmentary lines explode into a line of flight, but the line of flight is part of the rhizome. These lines never cease to refer to one another, which is why a dualism or dichotomy can never be assumed, even in the rudimentary form of good and bad. A rupture is made, a line of flight is traced, yet there is always the risk of finding along it organizations that restratify everything, formations that restore power to a signifier, attributions that reconstitute a subject . . . (Deleuze and Guattari, 1983a:18)

Desire is implicated at every point in the rhizomic web, and is referred immediately to every other point with which it is interconnected. There is never a dichotomy or duality, because there is no separation (displacement) between either the elements of a system or the positionings of an individual subject. All are endlessly interrelated. Cross-references and new linkages continually form and reform, producing new meanings and new discursive and material practices. It is this concept of desire that informs the contemporary cyborg consciousness. It also derives from and provides the context for the work of Michel Foucault.

## Foucault

While all of Foucault's work has been influential, the two books most closely associated with contemporary work on 'the body' are *Discipline and Punish: The Birth of the Prison* (first published in France in 1975) and *The History of Sexuality Volume One: An Introduction* (first published in France in 1976). In their introduction to Foucault's work, *A Foucault Primer: Discourse, Power and the Subject* (1993), McHoul and Grace provide useful summaries of both books (McHoul and Grace, 1993:66–76, 76–90). They begin their synopsis of *Discipline and Punish* with the following oft-quoted lines from the chapter called 'Panopticism':

> Our society is one not of spectacle, but of surveillance; under the surface of images, one invests bodies in depth; behind the great abstraction of exchange, there continues the meticulous, concrete training of useful forces; the circuits of communication are the supports of an accumulation and a centralization of

> knowledge; the play of signs defines the anchorages of power; it is not that the beautiful totality of the individual is amputated, repressed, altered by our social order, it is rather that the individual is carefully fabricated in it, according to a whole technique of forces and bodies. (Foucault, 1979:217)

After summarising Foucault's survey of the techniques used in the production of the disciplined body, they conclude that 'to attribute to Foucault a "theory" of embodiment is to reduce his thesis on power to its least interesting dimension' (McHoul and Grace, 1993:73). Instead they argue that Foucault's interest is in questions such as 'What is our historical present? What are the institutions and systems of knowledge that critical theorists think that they can readily identify? What are the relationships between them within particular ensembles which characterise our present epoch?' (ibid.:73–4). They are doubtless correct to situate Foucault's study of the disciplining of the body in the context of theoretical concerns which continue to occupy him throughout his work. However, it must be noted also that *Discipline and Punish* has been enormously useful as a specific study of the ways in which the body is 'fabricated' within a particular social order. For many people it has provided ways of beginning to think about the body not as something neutral and natural, but as socially (re)produced and inscribed according to specific practices and discourses. As McHoul and Grace comment, although Foucault's particular focus was the prison system, his analysis might be extended to other institutional sites such as 'schools, hospitals, military centres, psychiatric institutions, administrative apparatuses, bureaucratic agencies, police forces, and so on' (ibid.:66).

In *The History of Sexuality Volume One* Foucault analyses what he calls the 'species body, the body imbued with the mechanics of life and serving as the basis of the biological processes' (Foucault, 1981:139). Whereas *Discipline and Punish* deals with an '*anatomo-politics of the human body*', *The History of Sexuality Volume One* outlines a '*biopolitics of the population*', the two politics constituting 'the twin poles around which the organization of power over life was deployed' (ibid.:139). Foucault explores the operation of this biopolitics, noting particularly the role of sexuality. Sexuality,

Foucault suggests, is not a site of repression in human behaviour. Quite the reverse, it is one of the most powerful technologies for the production of particular kinds of bodies:

> Sexuality must not be thought of as a kind of natural given which power tries to hold in check, or as an obscure domain which knowledge tries gradually to uncover. It is the name that can be given to a historical construct: not a furtive reality that is difficult to grasp, but a great surface network in which the stimulation of bodies, the intensification of pleasures, the incitement to discourse, the formation of special knowledges, the strengthening of controls and resistances, are linked to one another, in accordance with a few major strategies of knowledge and power. (ibid.:105–6)

Foucault specifies the various strategies by which the individual is implicated in this network of stimulation and pleasures and knowledges—as, for example, in the confessional. These are not strategies of containment, a means of socially controlling a chaotic natural sexuality, a sexual excess. Instead, such strategies produce that sexuality, that excess, as well as those individual subjectivities which are marked, inscribed, and fabricated within its bio-power.

This work on sexuality should also be contextualised in relation to Foucault's ongoing concern with the nature and disposition of power. As McHoul and Grace point out, Foucault was interested not just in the specifics of the confessional, but in the fact that such a technology is used at all and what it tells us about the institutions of our society (McHoul and Grace, 1993:90). Furthermore, they note that the knowledge produced by this technology 'may or may not be "true". The important point is that the technology is *effective* in producing what is considered as truth' (ibid). The specific focus of Foucault's enquiry leads, once again, to analyses of those networks of power relations in which the individual is produced, and with important consequences for studies of the production and fabrication of 'the body', as for example in work on the 'nature' of different sexualities, or on the elision or omission of certain sexualities (such as female).

In many instances the writings of Foucault—whether a specific project or the theoretical enquiries of which those researches are part—will be a referent in the following fuller explanations of many of these issues and ideas. Politicised critiques of the mind/body dualism, together with postmodern reconceptualisations of the 'body', constitute the context within which Foucault's work has been read and used. At the same time, that work has provided the theoretical framework within which such critiques and reworkings have been received and used.

All of this forms the context for the study of recent writings on 'the body', which during the 1980s replaced 'desire' as a focus of critical attention. The next chapter begins the study of recent writings on the body by focusing on gender and sexualities.

2

# (En)acting, (Per)forming Gender: Bodies, Sexes, Sexualities

Much of the recent theoretical and philosophical interest in the body was generated by feminists attempting to understand and to explicate the ways in which women are marginalised and even reviled within contemporary western society. For these analysts, the links between women or femininity and the body were crucial. What they discovered was that the body is equally marginalised and reviled in western thought. As the negative 'other' of the mind or consciousness, it becomes the marginalised term. In western thought this dichotomy is replicated in the terms 'man' and 'woman'. Consequently, the relationship between 'man' and 'woman' is homologous with that between 'mind' and 'body': as mind is to body, so man is to woman. Feminist writers also located in this simple (or rather simplistic) equivalence the grounds for many of those inequitable attitudes and practices in which men and women are socially implicated. The equation of women with the body, for instance, was combined in Christian thought with negative attitudes to the body, fostered particularly by St Paul and St Augustine. Consequently, women were equated with not only the physical (at the exclusion of the intellectual or spiritual or both), but also with attributes associated with the body under this particular regime of thought—notably, evil, corruption, deceitfulness, temptation and decay. Effectively, feminist investigations into the conceptualisation of women and femininity in contemporary western thought resulted in analyses of how it had conceptualised the body.

In this chapter I am going to consider a number of different approaches to the body by theorists concerned with the constitution of gender. It is not possible to reduce this work to a single narrative, since it derives from many different fields of enquiry, experiences and concerns. In fact, it is a strength rather than a weakness that tactical assaults on the hegemonic systems of heterosexist identification should derive simultaneously and ungovernably from so many unpredictable directions. This sampling of those enquiries ranges from feminist critiques of the 'generic' body to recent theoretical revaluations of terms such as 'sex' and 'gender', and draws attention to confrontations with specific uses (metaphorical and technological) made of female and male bodies. The final section deals specifically with one such appropriation of the body, namely as a signifier of (re)production. The technological management of reproduction can be seen as one of the most powerful contemporary assaults on the specific nature and power of the feminine. Historically its roots are in the masculinisation of childbirth management, but there is also a long history of masculine usage of metaphors of pregnancy and parturition to describe intellectual production. This complex contestation and exploitation of maternity is a powerful example of the ways in which gendered embodiment is not just a matter of abstract delineations of identities. It is also incorporated semiotically into the discursive and material reproduction of western societies.

## Politicising the gendered body

One of the first points of intervention by feminist theorists in this process of (re)conceptualisation was the seemingly contradictory declaration that 'the body' (as a universal, general and generic category) is male. Feminist theorists were concerned at the philosophical and practical implications of the fact that, whenever the body is abstractly thought of, it so often assumes masculine characteristics—despite the fact that the body is aligned metaphorically with the feminine. Is the reason for this seeming contradiction to be found in that 'public' domain in which this gendering of the body so clearly disadvantages women? For in western thought, 'public' and 'private' are aligned with other dichotomies such as mind/body and male/female. Thus 'female' comes to be aligned with both 'body' and 'private'; 'male' is aligned with 'mind' and 'public'. Feminist theorists, deconstructionists and post-structuralist theorists have long since challenged these dichotomies, showing just how provisional they are. It can be argued that those rigid classifications which constitute each term of the binaries simply do not exist; instead, one term is constituted by the repression of the other, and in a move which places the marginalised term at the very heart of the definition of the dominant. Nevertheless, as a set of strategic metaphors, these dichotomies continue to exist. Consequently, it has been particularly important for feminists to deconstruct them.

When the body is located in the public domain—when we are discussing the body that works, travels on public transport, drives cars, and plays sport—then both materially and practically it is assumed to be male. Predominantly, public (and arguably even private) buildings are built for male bodies, as are public conveyances, technologies and equipment. The particular sizes and shapes and needs of female bodies have not been attended to. Instead, the male body is constituted as some kind of 'universal', and women's particular needs—if attended to at all—are figured in relation to that universal ideal. This affects the ease with which women go about their everyday activities, whether their work centres on the home or outside it. For example, catching a bus is difficult if the bus steps are calibrated for people whose average height is much greater than yours, and if the design of the seats is such that you may well slide off them when the bus moves around corners if your weight does not attain some crucial level. If designers and architects now consider these inequities much more seriously than they have done in the past, it is often because of critiques by female members of those professions. This inequity was the product of a common assumption that the body is universally male. It had first to be recognised and brought to public attention before remedial action could be taken.

Similar inequities operate in the workplace, where conditions of employment assume all bodies are male. At one time there was even a push from within the women's movement to accept this notion of a universally undifferentiated body, since to do so might avoid the biology-as-destiny thinking which had for so long restricted women's access to jobs and training. It was soon recognised, however, that this assumption of a universal body radically disadvantaged women, since it failed to provide for specifically feminine attributes such as menstruation, pregnancy, breast-feeding and menopause. Not all of these specifically feminine considerations are yet recognised in labour relations. Nevertheless, there are now industrial provisions that concede the existence of pregnancy and childbirth, and partially acknowledge their value. Such provisions could not even be thought of when the industrial body was assumed to be male.

It may be claimed that the male body taken for granted in all these situations is not equally valid for all men. Seeing that the male body assumed in so many areas of domestic and industrial life is a specific male body—able-bodied, youthful to middle aged, middle class and Anglo-Saxon—it therefore disadvantages men who do not fit that particular profile. The recent provision of wheelchair access to many buildings is a further recognition of the limitations of that specificity. In terms of gender differences, the first step in recognising that western thought has operated with a universal or generic body every bit as particular and inequitable as the universal or generic pronoun ('he') came with investigations into problems faced by women in negotiating their everyday lives.

One consequence of this investigation and the political interventions it subsequently enabled was a revaluation of the theoretical distinction between 'sex' and 'gender', which had been used by many liberal feminists to explain the ways in which 'feminine' and 'masculine' behaviours were produced and enacted. This distinction was first proposed by Robert Stoller in a study of transsexualism called *Sex and Gender* (1968), in which he was concerned to dissociate biological sex from types of behaviour deemed 'masculine' and 'feminine'. For Stoller, 'sex' specifies biological attributes, whereas 'gender' refers to social behaviour. In this way Stoller hoped to relativise the relationship between the two, suggesting that 'gender' is a learned set of behaviours not related to biological essence. For feminists, Stoller's distinction seemed particularly useful. For if femininity could be conceptualised as a set of behaviours produced by social interactions—capable therefore of being changed—biology could no longer be equated with destiny. This gave women a way of combating the essentialism of sexist arguments that women are 'naturally' incapable of performing all kinds of social roles because of the exigencies of their biology. More recently it has also enabled women and men to argue against that complementary sexist essentialising of men which equates masculinity with aggression and competitiveness. Strategically, this distinction between 'sex' and 'gender' has enabled an important political intervention by freeing women and men to reconceptualise themselves and their behaviours. Unfortunately, however, its use has also led to the conceptualisation of the body as a kind of neutral space, a blank slate on which the acculturated meanings of gender are written.

This neutral reading of the body was soon recognised as inadequate, not only in a strictly theoretical or philosophical sense, but also with respect to the political aims of those using the sex/gender distinction. A particular problem was its continuing support for the notion of a 'generic' body that is implicitly male. It could not explain, for instance, why it is that when women operate in positions of authority they are heard and perceived differently from men in similar positions. After all, if gender were a purely discursive construct not connected with particular kinds of bodies, then why should women positioned in discursive contexts formerly associated with men be perceived or heard differently from men? And yet they are. Media treatments of women generally—but particularly of women in positions of power, such as politicians—amply demonstrate this differential at work. For example, the infamous vilification of Margaret Thatcher as the Iron Lady and Attila the Hen show how stereotypes of gender can be used to attack a professional and powerful woman. This happens very rarely if at all to male politicians. How often is a male politician criticised for not being sufficiently manly? Yet female politicians constantly deal with attacks that challenge their femininity rather than their policies and values. It is as if the female body is itself the greatest provocation to the voting public. So, for women, the elision of the body from considerations of gender is simply not politically viable.

Furthermore, if sex is perceived as neutral, then what sex—what body—is accounted for in legislation written to cover a whole range of social and work practices? Is there a neutral body which becomes pregnant? Once again we are returned to that 'generic' (masculine) body, which disadvantages all women and a great number of men. So even although the sex/gender distinction had served as a useful political and discursive practice for some years, it seemed itself to require a radical revaluation.

## (En)acting gender: bodies, sexes, sexualities

The interrogation of the sex/gender distinction developed at least in part out of women's lived experience—as wage-earners and home managers, in public spaces and institutions. Another perspective on the sex/gender debate comes from post-structuralist feminists, whose work engages with the problems of identity politics and also with the exigencies of such descriptors as feminine and masculine, 'female' and 'male' (see Butler, 1990; McNay, 1992).

Judith Butler's influential work refers back to Joan Riviere's essay, 'Womanliness as a Masquerade', in which Riviere suggests that not only do women adopt womanliness as a masquerade to stave off male jealousy and reprisal, but also that womanliness is itself a masquerade: 'The reader may now ask how I define womanliness or where I draw the line between genuine womanliness and the "masquerade." My suggestion is not, however, that there is any such difference; whether radical or superficial, they are the same thing' (Riviere, 1986:38). This claim opens up questions of 'authenticity' which Riviere herself deals with in the following sentence. In some more or less radical sense, she suggests, women necessarily adopt a mask which protects them from the reprisals of men for any incursions into the power appropriated by men; that mask is womanliness. She does not specifically consider the issue of what lies beneath the mask, what is covered in the spectacle or masquerade of womanliness. Judith Butler subsequently uses the notion of 'masquerade' in order to radically reassess the ways in which sex, gender and sexualities are configured. The indeterminacy of Riviere's formulation—which works to prevent simple identifications on the basis of an essential(ist) masculinity or femininity (for what is behind the mask?)—becomes a key point in Butler's analysis. Indeed, Riviere's claim provides her with a base from which to argue that there is no such thing as a natural and essential(ist) sex, sexuality, gender, or body, because all are implicated in regimes of power and knowledge like those identified by Foucault in his study of the history of sexuality:

> For Foucault, the body is not 'sexed' in any significant sense prior to its determination within a discourse through which it becomes invested with an 'idea' of natural or essential sex. The body gains meaning within discourse only in the context of power relations. Sexuality is an historically specific organization of power, discourse, bodies, and affectivity. As such, sexuality is understood by Foucault to produce 'sex' as an artificial concept which effectively extends and disguises the power relations responsible for its genesis. (Butler, 1990:92)

Butler uses this understanding of Foucault to problematise the relationship between sex and gender. Rather than assuming that sex is a natural and biological characteristic, Butler argues that in a sense it is subordinate to gender. For Butler, gender is the discursive practice which subsequently constitutes bodies as 'naturally' sexed. The discursive practice of gender—the categorising of individuals as either male or female—is essential in western society; as Ursula Le Guin writes in *The Left Hand of Darkness*: 'What is the first question we ask about a new-born baby?' (Le Guin, 1981:85). But although gender produces the notion of a prediscursive category of sex as part of its regulatory function, there is in fact no pre-existent 'sex' outside the discursive practice of gender. Butler then goes on to examine the implications of this insight for identities of sex and sexuality which are based in particular readings and perceptions of the body.

Like Foucault, Butler traces the production of male and female bodies as 'discrete and asymmetrical oppositions' (Butler, 1990:17) to the dominance of heterosexual desire. She notes that heterosexual desire constitutes part of a cultural matrix in which only certain kinds of identities, realised in particular bodies, can exist. Other possibilities, other identities, and other kinds of bodies are effectively suppressed. Instead, the two identities—male and female, masculine and feminine—are stabilised and rendered coherent as the guarantee and mark of a dominant heterosexuality. Many recent studies have demonstrated the ways in which, for example, particular medical and psychoanalytic regimes (among others) have been mobilised to ensure the maintenance of that dichotomy, and therefore of the supposedly coherent and integrated identities which constitute it (Foucault, 1981; Gallagher and Laquer, 1987; Featherstone, Hepworth and Turner, 1991; Shilling, 1993). As Butler notes: 'Gender is the repeated stylization of the body, a set of repeated acts within a highly rigid regulatory frame that congeal over time to produce the appearance of substance, of a natural sort of being' (Butler, 1990:33). She then problematises this 'natural sort of being' by an analysis of Foucault's reading of the case of the hermaphrodite, Herculine Barbin.

Foucault published a Preface to an edition of the diaries of Herculine Barbin, whose life seemed to exemplify those regimes of sexuality he himself had theorised. Before Barbin's hermaphroditism is discovered, Foucault sees her living an almost utopian existence, outside the law of compulsory heterosexuality and its constitutive genders, bodies, sexes and sexualities. Instead, she is free to play with the multiplicities and disruptions produced by her bodily confrontation with heterosexism. When Barbin's hermaphroditism is revealed by her doctor, she is compelled by law to dress as a man and to attempt to configure herself as masculine. This Foucault sees as her regulation by the law of heterosexism, which sexes her as male. Butler's critique of this interpretation of Barbin's situation rests on what she sees as Foucault's failure to recognise that the pleasures in which Barbin has been involved while 'unsexed' are themselves 'always already embedded in the pervasive but inarticulate law and, indeed, generated by the very law they are said to defy' (ibid.:98). That is, Barbin's pleasures can be read romantically as multiple and disruptive only within the context of the law of heterosexism. Foucault's reading seems to convey a scenario in which an originally unfettered (unsexed) Barbin revelled in her multiple pleasures. Butler counters this with a more complex reading in which Barbin's bodily ambiguity in the eyes of the law was a source of both liberation and distress—a distress which culminated in her suicide. For Butler, Barbin's diaries 'are subjection and defiance at once' (ibid.:105). She concludes:

> Herculine can never embody that law precisely because s/he cannot provide the occasion by which that law naturalizes itself in the symbolic structures of anatomy. In other words, the law is not simply a cultural imposition on an otherwise natural heterogeneity; the law requires conformity to its own notion of 'nature' and gains its legitimacy through the binary and asymmetrical naturalization of bodies in which the Phallus, though clearly not identical with the penis, nevertheless deploys the penis as its naturalized instrument and sign. (ibid:106)

There is no 'natural heterogeneity' for Butler, no natural or prediscursive state of Pan-like revelry to which the body has at some time belonged. Instead, Barbin's diaries and the trajectory of her life confirm the power of the law of heterosexism to inscribe and to delimit the possibilities of embodiment.

Barbin's hermaphroditism and its consequences may serve rather as an example of the ways in which gender is inscribed on the body as the guarantee of its 'lawfulness'. Other practices currently seen as culturally determined might be reconceptualised in this light. The controversial custom of female circumcision is also a means by which bodies are inscribed as 'lawfully' gendered, and as recognisably sexed. This is not to say that such practices are bound to continue. In order to understand their significance, however, it is also necessary to understand the disruption that their non-continuance would cause to the community in which they operate. Non-circumcised women appear equally as disruptive and threatening in these communities as Barbin did in hers. They would seem not only improperly gendered but also aberrantly sexed, in so far as their sexual morphology itself would not conform to social and legal expectations. Butler reads the work of Monique Wittig as demonstrating that '"sex" is the reality effect of a violent process that it concealed by that very effect' (ibid.:114). The production of the 'natural' sex by surgical intervention might well confirm that reading—that is, when 'aberrantly sexed' bodies are surgically altered after birth in order to (re)construct them in the image of an acceptable sexed embodiment. And this conclusion may well apply to more commonplace 'naturalised' interventions in the west, such as male circumcision.

Butler then considers the consequences of heterosexist assumptions about a correspondence between gender and sex—specifically between the behaviours and practices which constitute a recognisable gender identity, and the sex on which those gendered behaviours are assumed to be based. (She refers to Monique Wittig's essay, 'One is Not Born a Woman'.)

> Sex is taken as an 'immediate given,' 'a sensible given,' 'physical features,' belonging to a natural order. But what we believe to be a physical and direct perception is only a sophisticated and mythic construction, an 'imaginary formation,' which reinterprets physical features (in themselves as neutral as others but marked by a social system), through the network of relationships in which they are perceived. (ibid.:114)

Butler goes on to discuss Wittig's view that language shapes perception through its mediation of the relationships in which bodies are perceived and realised. A corollary of Wittig's view is that '"men" and "women" are political categories, and not natural facts' (ibid.:115). Although Butler critiques the homogeneity of Wittig's conceptualisation of heterosexuality, she nevertheless uses Wittig's work as a catalyst for her own writings on the subversive deployment of naturalised notions of identity (such as 'men' and 'women') by gay and lesbian subjects.

Heterosexism treats as confrontational the non-correspondence of bodies—constituted as gendered, and sexed in a particular way—with their 'natural' and 'lawful' objects of desire, and their subsequent deployment of bodily surfaces and orifices. Butler proposes 'drag' as an explicit and performative means by which this non-correspondence—and the questions it prompts—is achieved. Most seriously, drag challenges the assumed coherence or integrity of 'interior' and 'exterior', which is perceived as the mark of a viable subjectivity. As Butler observes: '*In imitating gender, drag implicitly reveals the imitative structure of gender itself—as well as its contingency*' (ibid.:137). Butler concludes by noting that since gender is a performative act (that is, not a reified concept but a practice) which gains credence through repetition, the possibilities of gender-transformation lie in disrupting such repetition. And since sex is produced by these gender identities, then the 'naturalised' sex they assumed will be simultaneously disrupted. This process has important implications for our perceptions of the body.

Butler derives a definition of the body in part from *Purity and Danger* (1966) by the anthropologist, Mary Douglas: 'the body is not a "being," but a variable boundary, a surface whose permeability is politically regulated, a signifying practice within a cultural field of gender hierarchy and compulsory heterosexuality . . .' (Butler, 1990:139). This stimulating work on the relationship between sex and gender is particularly important for feminists and others attempting to theorise the inscription of gender on bodies and to constitute those bodies as part of a network of interactions through which they are subsequently perceived as 'beings'. Such work subverts simple kinds of identity politics based on male and female bodies since the interrogation by writers such as Butler of how sex is constituted denies that sex has a universal and essentialising significance. On the one hand, this may seem politically problematic in disavowing a potential source of solidarity. On the other hand, however, Butler (and others such as Lois McNay, Teresa de Lauretis and Donna Haraway) warn against the adoption or even the use of notions of identity which elide differences and tend to lock individuals into socially dominant categories. Ignoring differences of race between white and black women, for example, almost inevitably privileges white women in most contexts. As McNay comments:

> An advantage of an ethics based on such a relational idea of identity is that it encourages us to think of difference in terms of its construction through the social realm . . . it multiplies the points of resistance to the myriad of relations of inequality and domination that constitute the social field . . . as Sawicki puts it, 'if we redefine our differences, discover new ways of understanding ourselves and each other, then our differences are less likely to be used against us.' (McNay, 1992:110)

So rather than suppressing solidarity, the notion of identity as something displaced across a variety of different positionings (race, class, ethnicity, age, gender and sexuality) offers opportunities for more interventions, subversions and other oppositional activities. Bodies constituted within this interlocking network of identities and their constitutive discourses are not constrained by identifications that may otherwise elide or conceal the specificities of their experience of any of their constitutive positionings and its associated inscriptions. Identities of gender, for example, will not ignore those differences of race, class or ethnicity that are suppressed by the dominant (often hegemonic) discourse. Such elisions have been the source of much dissatisfaction with the women's movement, where the specificities of a white, middle-class, heterosexual, and Anglo woman's existence came to be the yardstick or point of identity for all women. That not only omitted the embodied experience of all other women, but also aligned those feminists implicitly with bourgeois, Anglocentric, homophobic and white supremacist discourses. This was understood only when women of colour, lesbians and working-class women began to contest their prejudicial positioning, and to argue *from the body* about their different experiences. To analogise from an earlier argument, a white woman and a black woman in a similar institutional position, speaking the same discourse, are not perceived in the same way. Relationally-constituted bodies, however, are not confined by such simplistic positioning. Furthermore, they are able to form strategic alliances which enable them to contest hegemonic values, discourses and practices. Mary Douglas points out that social order is created by 'exaggerating the differences between within and without, above and below, male and female, with and against . . .' (quoted in Butler, 1990:131). By relativising the terms, 'male' and 'female', and by implicating them within a network of discourses and practices that inflect their significance differently at any one time and place, it is possible to challenge both the gendering of bodies and those assumptions about sex and sexuality that correspond to it.

## (Re)production: gender in performance

The reproductive capacity or power of women occupies a unique position in the construction of regimes for regulating sexuality, particularly through its medicalisation. It has also been one of the few specifically female capacities which men have long attempted in various ways to usurp, either metaphorically or, more recently, through technology. As such it offers fascinating insights into the practices of gendering.

One of the most striking uses of 'the body' is as a metaphor for the output of an artist: the body or corpus of her or his work. In attempting to understand this use of the term—which sits uncomfortably with the mind/body dichotomy, rendering the artist's work non-intellectual or non-spiritual—we are led to another complex of meanings in which the body is implicated, and which concern production and reproduction. In the 1580s the English poet Sir Philip Sidney wrote in this way about his struggles to write:

> Thus, great with child to speak, and helpless in my throes,
> Biting my trewand pen, beating myself for spite,
> 'Fool,' says my muse to me, 'look in thy heart and write.'
> (quoted in Friedman, 1991:371)

This appropriation of the peculiarly female ability to bear children is not uncommon in English literature. Susan Stanford Friedman discusses the figurative construction of writing as parturition in 'Creativity and the Childbirth Metaphor' (1991):

> This wordplay reveals not only currents of unconscious thought as Sigmund Freud has described but also the structures of patriarchy that have divided *labor* into men's *production* and women's *reproduction*. Underlying these words is the familiar dualism of mind and body, a key component in Western patriarchal ideology. *Creation* is the act of mind that brings something new into existence. *Procreation* is the act of the body that reproduces the species. A man *conceives* an idea in his brain, while a woman *conceives* a baby in her womb, a difference highlighted by the post-industrial designation of the public sphere as man's domain and the private sphere as woman's place. The *pregnant* body is necessarily female; the *pregnant* mind is the mental province of genius, most frequently understood to be inherently masculine. *Confinement* of men suggests imprisonment—indignities to, not the fulfillment of manhood. *Delivery* from confinement suggests the restoration of men's autonomy, not its death. *Confinement* of women, in contrast, alludes to the final stages of pregnancy before *delivery* into the bonds of

> maternity, the very joy of which has suppressed their individuality in patriarchy. (Friedman, 1991:373)

So this (metaphorical) use of the female body also tells us a great deal about (western heterosexist) masculine attitudes to women and children. First, it demonstrates an extraordinarily possessive attitude to children: they are the products of the father-artist's consciousness or subjectivity, 'conceived' by him, and of value as such. Once given 'birth' to, however, they are then immediately part of the public domain, requiring no further care or nurturing from the post-partum father. This is radically deconstructive of bourgeois heterosexist attitudes not only to child-care (men do not do it) but also to the reproductive power of women (men are jealous of it). Mary Shelley's *Frankenstein* (1818) can be read as a fictional exploration of this complex of attitudes. Victor Frankenstein's desperate struggle to create human life—his Promethean quest—can be read as another example of Sidney's attitude: to figure his work as equivalent to bodily reproduction, and thus to usurp that peculiarly feminine role. And when his creature is born —misshapen and ill conceived as it is (which is Shelley's own commentary perhaps on this masculine colonisation of the feminine) —his response is not that of the caring father; instead, he refuses to have anything to do with it. The creature himself attributes his own subsequent violence to this rejection by his creator/father. In other words, the heterosexist male, while jealous of the female power of reproduction, nevertheless eschews the responsibility for it. In a sense, this abdication of responsibility—the eschewing of the need to care for another embodied being (physically and bodily, as well as emotionally, spiritually and intellectually)—can be read as a measure of the abstraction involved in this metaphorical exploitation of the body, which entails no bodily realisation or impact. It may be argued also that only male artists can use this metaphor successfully since their male bodies distance them effectively from a metaphor that might relegate them otherwise to the realm of the body, the emotional, and the feminine.

As used in western societies, traditional dichotomies such as masculinity/femininity and intellectual/physical make it clear that masculine appropriations of the body for metaphorical purposes will never be more than playful. Ultimately they will be abandoned in favour of a conservative positioning in which masculinity is associated unequivocally with the intellectual. Metaphorical appropriations of the feminine power of reproduction are strictly conditional, therefore, on a simultaneous acknowledgment that the pregnancy being referred to is purely intellectual (productive), and not bodily (reproductive). Ironically (and as Mary Shelley's novel demonstrates), once the metaphor is actualised—in a move which those who propagate it would never condone—its deconstructive power is revealed. In a Derridean manoeuvre, the body is positioned as dominant in a dichotomy whose other term is mind/intellect/creativity. So the body and its metaphorical equivalents (female/femininity, emotion and reproduction) are revealed as the terms that underlie and thus inform the constitution of the creative masculine. In this system of equivalences, creative masculinity is dependent on the repression of the body and what it entails, namely femininity, emotion and reproduction.

Taking this a step further, what then is the role of the creative feminine? How is it constituted, and what relationship (metaphorical and otherwise) does it have to the body? As Cixous' chain of metaphors suggests, the feminine and woman are identified not with production but with reproduction, which in turn is considered a second-order act of creativity. As embodied subjects with the potential for reproduction, women find themselves positioned in this society as second-order producers—despite the fact that only they have the power to bodily (re)produce. Hence it is doubly ironic that male artists favour the use of this metaphor. Nor perhaps is it surprising that, in the artistic world, so much prestige and value is invested in distinguishing oneself as a 'creator' or 'producer' of unique works. This Romantic conception of the artist as a figure alone and outside society, supposedly independent of earlier times and texts, is based on the devaluing of any notion of 're-production', the copying of an earlier work. Recently, however, critical and artistic theory and practice have focused on this fetishisation of the 'new'. Every text, it is now argued, contains intertextual echoes of its prehistory. These link both the text and its producer into a network of production and (re)presentation that characterises a particular society and its cultures. In other words, contemporary critical and artistic theory and practice tend to assume that all textual activity is a matter of reproduction rather than production. In the hands of an individual artist, reproductive moves may be inflected in particular ways to produce something 'different', if not 'new'; simultaneously it will reflect on the practice of its own (re)production. This reconfiguration of discourses and their constitutive metaphors should lead to a revaluation of terms such as reproduction. Perhaps the contemporary focus on the body—in theoretical debate as well as in artistic practice—is part of this change. If so, we might then ask how it impacts on the position of the female artist.

Many of the strategies used to exclude and to marginalise female artists have been closely related to the body. For example, female art students in the nineteenth century were excluded from figure classes, even when the model was a woman, on the grounds that it was improper for them to see a naked body. Even where this overt prohibition did not exist, female students were often made so uncomfortable by the attitudes of instructors and male students to the female models—specifically, to their bodies—that they felt they were being driven from the classes. This kind of implicit discrimination has been reported very recently by students studying in the 1970s. In each case the body of the female model becomes a source of sexual speculation by male students, whose dismissive attitude to the (female) body and to sexuality is used to drive women out of their classes (Cranny-Francis, 1992:67). From an analogous situation, Dale Spender reports Erica Jong's memories of a visit to her writing class by a 'distinguished male critic' who pointed out to them the reasons why women cannot be writers: '"Women can't be writers. They don't know blood and guts, and puking in the streets, and fucking whores, and swaggering through Pigalle at 5:00 a.m. . . ."' (Spender, 1989:27). So in this estimation, women cannot be writers because they do not treat their bodies as instruments of power, as masculine heroes do. In place of the pregnant author we have here the instrumental penis/phallus which is seen as the proper instrument of creativity. Clearly, of course, this reasoning is spurious for many women are writers; yet several have written and spoken of its devastating effect on their self-esteem, as well as on their ability to receive training and to be published or exhibited (Russ, 1984; Spender, 1989; Cranny-Francis, 1992). In her study of the childbirth metaphor Friedman summarises one of the conclusions drawn by Gilbert and Gubar in *The Mad-Woman in the Attic*: 'the association of the pen and the paintbrush with the phallus in metaphors of creativity has resulted in an "anxiety of authorship" for aspiring women writers: to wield a pen is a masculine act that puts the woman writer at war with her body and her culture' (quoted in Friedman, 1991:371). It is interesting that this same motif was used recently in the illustration accompanying a review of books by a number of Australian women in the *Weekend Australian* (Cranny-Francis, 1991). So the only creative use of the body deemed valid in artistic production is either as an object of speculation and consumption (if female) or as an instrument (if male). As an instrument of the male will or intellect, the phallic pen is a conceptualisation that not only reinforces the mind/body dichotomy but also positions artistic production in the realm of the masculine as a purely intellectual or spiritual affair. This situation will remain for as long as the body is equated with the feminine, which is equated in turn with reproduction as distinct from production. Yet most recent artistic practice and critical theory reject this valorisation, which secures the dominance of 'production' in western systems of value specifically by devaluing 'reproduction'. Both postmodernist and post-structuralist writings argue against the notion of production as an isolated, inspired and God-like creativity, preferring instead to think of production as intertextually connected with and through those cultures in which it is rooted. That kind of production is more like reproduction. Such writings constitute one means of changing the older dichotomising of production and reproduction. Theoretically, such a change should engender a different attitude to female artistry as well as to women in general. It should also change our attitudes to different forms of art and craft, whose status at present depends on their association with the body, or with the masculine and the feminine, or with both (Cranny-Francis, 1992:2–3).

When considering the bodily metaphors for artistic production, it is clearly important to look also at their real foundation in contemporary attitudes to pregnancy and childbirth. Feminist critics have written and spoken extensively about the ways in which women's bodily potential for pregnancy and childbirth has resulted in their marginalisation and exclusion. Most of this commentary has focused on the way in which society encourages women to become mothers—to the extent that those who do not are regarded as lacking in femininity and not fulfilling their 'natural' destiny—and yet simultaneously positions mothers as second-class citizens. This belittling of motherhood takes a variety of forms. The failure to provide public facilities for women and children is one example: access to public facilities for people with prams is often made almost impossible by long flights of stairs; rooms to change and to feed infants are difficult to find, and often extremely dirty. Another example is public disapproval for mothers who choose, however discreetly, to breast-feed a baby in public. And then there is the disadvantaging of women in all kinds of employment whose careers are disrupted in any way by the demands of pregnancy, childbirth and child-care. While there seems to be a general social demand that women bear children, there is an apparent paradoxic devaluation of both mothers and their children. This paradox is again based in the mind/body dichotomy, as inflected in a society dominated by bourgeois capitalist practices.

Such contradictions are perhaps best illustrated in contemporary western attitudes to conception and childbirth. For many feminists one of the most disturbing features of contemporary medical practice has been the medicalisation of childbirth. The history of the medical treatment of childbirth in the west demonstrates how male medical practitioners usurped the role of the midwife, which traditionally had been a female profession. Medicalisation introduced practices which have been criticised recently as detrimental to women, and most obviously in the way in which control over the birthing process has been taken away from the very women who are giving birth. Pregnant women are pathologised as 'ill', and their 'case' handed over to a practitioner who is often male. Endemic in this medicalisation is an extremely disturbing attitude to the body. A pregnant woman is often treated as a receptacle, a 'walking womb', and an object rather than a subject with her own needs and desires. She is reduced, via her physicality, her body, to the status of object which can then be treated in whatever way the medical professional deems fit—even if that means scheduling a caesarean delivery to fit in with the proverbial golf game. Throughout the pregnancy, birth and antenatal period, women report being made to feel as if their bodies are recalcitrant or gross or incompetent because they do not fit some social or medical 'norm'. The terms used for various 'medical conditions' in pregnancy reveal such attitudes: for example, a woman who experiences difficulty in carrying a baby to term because of previous damage to her cervix is said to have an 'incompetent cervix'. Other practices in childbirth, such as enforced enemas, have been performed mainly for the benefit of medical practitioners, who do not want to be confronted with disturbing signs of a woman's physicality. Kristeva's work on the notion of 'abjection' is useful in dealing with responses of this kind (see Kristeva, 1982). Social attitudes to the post-partum body are often highly distressing for women. Rather than being praised as a sign of fertility (as it is in some cultures), the soft and often fat post-partum female body is ridiculed in the west as a sign of weakness or incompetence. Although some sections of western cultures (for example, the working class) may resist this valorisation, it nevertheless remains dominant. And, as so many critics have noted, the ostracising of large-bodied females is a specific rejection of the body and its physicality. The male body, by contrast, is somehow elided in the constitution of the male/masculine as 'mind'.

Another way in which the female body can be medically 'managed' in conception and childbirth is via reproductive technologies. Again this is something which has recently received a great deal of attention. Issues of concern include the implicit downgrading of any woman involved in *in vitro* fertilisation procedures to the status of receptacle, although one might also consider the comparable effects on the men involved in such practices, who find themselves treated as more or less competent sperm-banks. The bodies of the people involved (and most writing has concentrated on the women) are subjected to medical procedures and regimes that are almost certainly alienating. At the expense of their emotional, intellectual and spiritual well-being, such women are seen as pawns in a much larger game of medical research and scientific adventurism. The fact that only 5–10 per cent of them conceive in these conditions is seen as proof of the medical irresponsibility and social hypocrisy involved. In a disturbing late twentieth-century revision of *Frank-*

*enstein,* once again men (for the majority of researchers, medical practitioners and drug company managers in this field are male) are attempting to usurp the (re)productive role of women. The drive to develop these technologies seems to be a drive to achieve total control over the body, and particularly the female as body. As Cait Featherstone writes: 'The men without skin want our skin' (Featherstone, 1991:85). The same concern characterises recent critiques of procedures used to impregnate women who are past the usual age for bearing children, particularly post-menopausal women who are implanted with a fertilised ovum and then have their bodies chemically manipulated in order to provide a viable environment for the growing foetus. Represented as a compassionate response to the desires of a woman who has not previously had a child, it may nevertheless be a monstrous manipulation of her by a medical establishment obsessed with a desire to dominate the body.

In surveying such writings about reproduction and contemporary attitudes to conception and childbirth, one notes that a certain essentialism has crept back into their arguments. 'Women' are seen as being manipulated and exploited by these practices (metaphorical as well as medical and technological), and often for the gratification of 'men'. Yet it is undeniable that among humans the ability to bodily grow and give birth to a child is (so far at least) a distinctly female capacity. Moreover, it has been incorporated into those regimes which disadvantage women in all public contexts by presenting it as a source not of power but of vulnerability. Implicitly, if not openly, men are coerced into compliance with these uses because of the advantages they seem to offer, whether as an eloquent way of discussing the pangs of artistic creation, or as the spirit of scientific adventure associated with new technologies such as IVF. On the one hand, this exploration of the use of reproduction demonstrates very vividly the alignment of the body with femininity. After all, the role of the male partner in the reproductive procedures —metaphorical or bodily—is consistently ignored. The only exceptions are cases like the Maileresque diatribe discussed earlier, where instrumental masculinity ('puking . . . fucking . . . swaggering') is constructed as a necessary precondition for creativity (quoted in Spender, 1989:27). Yet even here the 'fucking' which may lead to reproduction is associated with more clearly bodily imperatives such as puking, which are metaphorically aligned in turn with the feminine. Perhaps this is a Maileresque version of the Muse? The gendering of such metaphors, as well as their elisions, confirms what Butler and others identify as the heterosexist production of 'woman' and 'man'. On the other hand, exploration of the uses of reproduction might also suggest new ways of reconfiguring this function, which in Butler's terms will open up its subversive potential. For example, the alignment of maternal reproduction (conception, pregnancy, and childbirth) with heterosexuality is now skewed by lesbian maternity. Again a different conceptualisation of the male role in conception, pregnancy and childbirth might radically confront heterosexist assumptions. Not only are there precedents for this (other societies have configured the male role differently), but the men's movement is also attempting to reconstruct the familiar heterosexist idea of the male as instrumental only. Butler notes of Mary Douglas:

> Her analysis suggests that what constitutes the limit of the body is never merely material, but that the surface, the skin, is systemically signified by taboos and anticipated transgressions; indeed, the boundaries of the body become, with her analysis, the limits of the social *per se*. (Butler, 1990:131)

Bearing in mind this reconceptualisation of the body, it is possible to reconfigure the whole process of conception, pregnancy, childbirth, nurturing, as one of the means by which heterosexism has maintained the dichotomised views of man/woman, mind/body, instrument/receptacle, and production/reproduction that currently dominate western understanding of gender and its embodiment. And that reconfiguration itself exemplifies the kind of subversive process to which Butler refers. Like drag, contemporary conceptualisations of reproduction can be seen as part of the masquerade that constitutes not only womanliness but also manliness. Butler's somewhat utopian conclusion articulates the potential in current theoretical debates to transform the current binaristic inscription of bodies as male and female:

> If identities were no longer fixed as the premises of a political syllogism, and politics no longer understood as a set of practices

derived from the alleged interests that belong to a set of ready-made subjects, a new configuration of politics would surely emerge from the ruins of the old. Cultural configurations of sex and gender might then proliferate or, rather, their present proliferation might then become articulable within the discourses that establish intelligible cultural life, confounding the very binarism of sex, and exposing its fundamental unnaturalness. (ibid.:149)

3

# Embodying the Other: Inscriptions of Race and Ethnicity

The previous chapter focused on the ways in which the body is figured in social constructions of gender, and on difficulties encountered in attempting to construct an identity politics based simply on gender. This is seen as problematic not only because it tends to reinforce conservative versions of gender identity, but also because it works to elide differences between individuals who otherwise might be classified as belonging socially to the same 'gender'. In particular, the elision of the experiences of other than middle-class Anglo women was a serious critique of the women's movement—just as, it might argued, the elision of women's experience is a common failing of many socialist movements. Instead such specificities as race, ethnicity, class and age should be recognised and used not to divide individuals, but to provide the grounds for strategic alliances which will enable them to act together without necessarily suppressing or denying their differences.

This postmodern project is not without detractors, of course. bell hooks writes that she is not surprised 'when black folks respond to the critique of essentialism, especially when it denies the validity of identity politics by saying, "Yeah, it's easy to give up identity, when you got one"' (hooks, 1990:28). Yet she maintains her belief that the postmodern interrogation of identity and subjectivity as constructs is crucial for African-Americans, because it enables them to challenge those essentialist stereotypes that persist in Anglo culture and are the source of much racist oppression. It is also important, however, to raise here another issue discussed by hooks in connection with identity and difference, and that it is the ease with which 'we' all recognise the 'other' in studies of 'otherness'.

Australia's geographical position in the South-east Asian Pacific region places its Anglo-Celtic and European populations as uniquely 'other' in relation to the indigenous peoples of Australia, the Melanesian and Polynesian peoples of the Pacific, and the Asian peoples to Australia's north. In a sense, if anyone is 'other' in this region it would seem to be the Anglo-Celtic and European Australians. Since this is a perspective rarely adopted by local scholars and researchers, it may be useful to ponder the reasons why. The elision of Anglo-Celtic and European otherness might be seen as a consequence of western global dominance. Western society in general has a major role—economically, politically, militarily—in the constitution of global affairs. And since western countries are predominantly a composite of Anglo, Celtic and European cultures, then it seems that western scholars in Australia tend to situate themselves globally, and to reproduce the notions of 'otherness' derived (however temporarily) from that positioning. Simultaneously, of course, this makes them complicit in the discourses which maintain the west as a powerful force in assuming itself to be the 'centre' of 'authority' and 'correctness'. As hooks suggests, the study of 'whiteness' would be a useful development. Western society might then be recognised as being equally as specific as 'other' cultures, having assumptions and prejudices of its own which only military and economic dominance has enabled it to represent as natural, inevitable, central or correct.

That being said, this chapter will now map two complementary developments. First, the ways in which western society constitutes particular positionings—that is, particular races and ethnicities—as 'other' to itself. And secondly, the ways in which dominant or mainstream positionings within western society are thereby and simultaneously constituted, maintained and reproduced. My particular focus will be on how this topography is mapped on to the body.

## Racial stereotyping and bodily inscription

In her essay on 'Postmodern Blackness', bell hooks writes of the ways in which colonial imperialist systems of thought construct black identity 'one-dimensionally in ways that reinforce and sustain white supremacy. This discourse created the idea of the "primitive" and promoted the notion of an "authentic" experience, seeing as "natural" those expressions of black life which conformed to a pre-existing pattern or stereotype' (hooks, 1990:28). Nobody aware of the ramifications of the western mind/body dichotomy will be surprised to witness here the constitution of black society and its cultures as a 'primitive' adjunct of the 'body' by comparison with a 'sophisticated' society whose cultures are correlated with the 'mind'. Consider the following passage from Joseph Conrad's novel, *Heart of Darkness* (1899):

> Now and then a boat from the shore gave one a momentary contact with reality. It was paddled by black fellows. You could see from afar the white of their eyeballs glistening. They shouted, sang; their bodies steamed with perspiration; they had faces like grotesque masks—these chaps; but they had bone, muscle, a wild vitality, an intense energy that was as natural and true as the surf along their coast. They wanted no excuse for being there. They were a great comfort to look at. (quoted in Moon, 1992:50)

Brian Moon quotes this passage in his glossary of *Literary Terms* (1992) to illustrate exactly the point being made here: that the black people in this passage are constructed in purely physical terms. They are constructed as bodies for visual consumption by a European narrator in a scopophiliac or voyeuristic process that establishes European authority in matters of commentary and judgement. So the constitution of the black rowers as manifestations of the physical (pure body) enables the elevation of the European as a manifestation of the intellectual (pure mind). This construction of non-whites as de-cultured and objectified bodies is a colonialist strategy, familiar in such forms of cultural production as novels, magazines, newspapers, films and television. The *National Geographic* magazine is a particularly striking example of this kind of cultural imperialism, whereby peoples from regions geographically or culturally 'remote' are primitivised by the camera, which gives them a bodily presence but never a voice. Furthermore, such images are often gendered in ways which load on to that embodied image of alterity or otherness an Augustinian fear and loathing of the body, and particularly of sexuality. At the same time, however, they constitute the gendered body of the other as a locus of desire. For many children and teenagers curious about bodies and sexuality, magazines like *National Geographic* constituted until fairly recently one of the few socially sanctioned sources of images of naked bodies. Yet because those bodies are always non-white, they are exactly the kind of fetishised image which Homi Bhabha deconstructs as stereotypical (Bhabha, 1990).

Discussing this sexualising of the stereotype, bell hooks begins by specifying the political function of rape in the maintenance of slave relations: 'black women's bodies were the discursive domain, the playing fields where racism and sexuality converged' (hooks, 1990:57). This intersection of race and sex, she writes, has always provided 'gendered metaphors for colonization':

> Free countries equated with free men, domination with castration, the loss of manhood, and rape—the terrorist act re-enacting the drama of conquest, as men of the dominating group sexually violate the bodies of women who are among the dominated. The intent of this act was to continually remind dominated men of their loss of power; rape was a gesture of symbolic castration. (ibid.:57)

So the bodies of the colonised are the grounds on which colonisation is maintained. Furthermore, she notes, this metaphorical production of the racial 'other' engenders another narrative, which again combines race and sex but in a different configuration: 'That story, invented by white men, is about the overwhelming desperate longing black men have to sexually violate the bodies of white women' (ibid.:58). And she quotes Michael Dyson's description of the black men in this scenario as '"peripatetic phalluses with unrequited desire for their denied object—white women"' (ibid.:58). The sources of this narrative are unclear, and possibly multiple. Is it a displacement of white guilt over the brutal treatment of black women or a containment strategy for coping with instances of interracial love? Whatever its provenance, it is a pervasive narrative in western society and white cultures. As a case in point, hooks cites Madonna's video, 'Like a Virgin', where the passion of the white woman (a subversive narrative in itself) is directed toward black men. Because this activates in viewers' minds the stereotype of the black male rapist, it undermines the subversive potential of the gender narrative (ibid.:60–1). Marcia Langton writes about the same narrative in an Australian film, *Jedda* (1955), which depicts a rebellious Aboriginal man, Marbuk, as an outlaw and the seducer of Jedda, a young Aboriginal woman who has come under the 'civilising' influence of a white family (Langton, 1993:45–8). Jedda's significance in this film is that she constitutes 'whiteness' by adopting the manners and morals—the civility—of the white settlers. Marbuk, by contrast, represents the life of the 'primitive' from which she has 'escaped'—a world of sensuality and passion. Because Marbuk is represented in terms of the body, his implicit seduction of Jedda identifies him as black-man-as-rapist in the narrative of which hooks writes.

This common narrative in western society motivates many textual constructions not only of black–white relations but also of relations between peoples of different ethnicities and classes. One of its most striking characteristics is its implicit evocation of both fear and desire. Langton writes of the possible appeal of Marbuk in these terms:

> Could there have been a secret identification with Jedda among the white women in the cinema audience? Might they have been captivated and fascinated by the story of Marbuk's sorcery and seduction, (silently subverting in the heat of the dark cinema the repressive patriarchy which they had to endure); a seduction so much more exciting than the Rock Hudson type of seduction in the Hollywood romance? (ibid.:48)

James Tiptree Jr (Alice Sheldon) describes the relationship between colonialist racism and sexism in several of her short stories, such as 'We Who Stole the *Dream*' and 'The Women Men Don't See' (Tiptree, 1975). In the latter a sexist male narrator, Donald

Fenton, an American, recalls his own fantasies about Mayan women, prompted by the sight of the male Mayan pilot:

> Our captain's classic Maya profile attracts my gaze: forehead sloping back from his predatory nose, lips and jaw stepping back below it. If his slant eyes had been any more crossed, he couldn't have made his license. That's a handsome combination, believe it or not. On the little Maya chicks in their minishifts with iridescent goop on those cockeyes, it's also highly erotic. Nothing like the oriental doll thing; these people have stone bones. (Tiptree, 1975:133)

Tiptree uses this passage to indicate the colonialist mentality which shapes Fenton's point of view. And she extrapolates that fundamentally colonialist sexism in exactly the ways that Langton and hooks describe. After his plane has made an emergency landing, and Fenton sets off with one of the American women passengers to look for help, his thoughts return to the Mayan pilot and his possible liaison with the woman's daughter: 'Captain Estéban's mahogany arms clasping Miss Althea Parsons' pearly body. Captain Estéban's archaic nostrils snuffling in Miss Parsons' tender neck. Captain Estéban's copper buttocks pumping into Althea's creamy upturned bottom . . . The hammock, very bouncy. Mayas know all about it' (ibid.:150).

Fenton's fantasies about Captain Estéban are an attempt to displace his own failure both as a rescuer (he injures himself and has to be carried by Mrs Parsons) and as a seducer (Mrs Parsons is not interested in him). By tracing this sexual and social pathology in Fenton, Tiptree describes the co-articulation of colonialism and sexism in the consciousness of a particular individual, and how it operates in his positioning of himself—against all evidence—as an authoritative voice. Furthermore, Tiptree's story begins to tease out that conjunction of desire and fear which motivates this subjectivity. Desire manifests itself in colonialist possessiveness towards the bodies of Mayan women, sexist possessiveness towards the American women, and the constitution of the Mayan pilot as a 'peripatetic phallus'. But in Fenton such desires are accompanied by fear of the women, of the extraterrestrials they encounter, of his own incompetence, of the jungle—in short, of the body.

Homi Bhabha theorises this complex of fear and desire in colonialist discourse in an article called 'The Other Question: Difference, Discrimination and the Discourse of Colonialism', first published in 1984. Using psychoanalytic theory, he investigates that concept of the 'stereotype', which theorists such as bell hooks recognise as essential to the production and maintenance under colonialism of racist attitudes and practices. In so doing, Bhabha challenges western notions of otherness:

> What is denied is any knowledge of cultural otherness as a differential *sign*, implicated in specific historical and discursive conditions, requiring construction in different practices or reading. The place of otherness is fixed in the west as a subversion of western metaphysics and is finally appropriated by the west as its limit-text, anti-west. (Bhabha, 1990:73)

In other words, 'otherness' is the negative test-case which enables western metaphysics to maintain its centrality as a mode of thought. The Derridean notion of *différance* can be seen as participating in the same practice through its denial of 'originality'. That is, if western metaphysics refuses any notion of difference which is not predicated on sameness, then it becomes implicated in the very practices which underlie colonialism. To avoid that problem, Bhabha thinks we need to constitute otherness not as a symbol (or stereotype) but as a sign of the complex social, political, historical, economic and libidinal conditions of existence.

The stereotype (symbol) works in a completely different way, being ahistorical, apolitical and asocial. The libidinal and economic conditions of existence of otherness as a symbol are both prescribed and proscribed. They are perceived as the 'natural' opposite and defining conditions of western dominance (in the form of sexual propriety and the bourgeois work ethic). They are inscribed on the bodies of those marked by this otherness (as sexual availability, sexual promiscuity or provocativeness, laziness and shiftlessness). As hooks notes, in the USA the bodies of black men and women were the grounds on which the racist discourse of slavery was enacted and inscribed as the possessed female body and the promiscuous male body. Similar constructions of otherness are embodied in representations of other colonised peoples, as Langton notes of indigenous Australians and Said of 'orientals'. Attempting to explicate the complex of fear and desire associated with these stereotypes, Bhabha observes how this narrative is based in part on the incorporation of traditional elites into colonial administrations: 'This sets up the native subject as a site of productive power, both subservient and always potentially seditious. What is increased is the visibility of the subject as an object of surveillance, tabulation, enumeration, and indeed, paranoia and fantasy' (ibid.:76).

Another motivation for this narrative may well be the kinds of interracial, interpersonal and sexual relationships discussed by hooks (hooks, 1990:57–8). Bhabha, however, sees this mixture of paranoia and fantasy as encapsulated in the stereotype, analysed by Edward Said in *Orientalism* (1978). Here Said describes the ways in which western literature reconfigures the oriental 'other' in more familiar terms:

> One tends to stop judging things either as completely novel or as completely well-known; a new median category emerges, a category that allows one to see new things, things seen for the first time, as versions of a previously known thing. In essence such a category is not so much a way of receiving new information as it is a method of controlling what seems to be a threat to some established view of things . . . The Orient at large, therefore, vacillates between the West's contempt for what is familiar and its shivers of delight in—or fear of—novelty. (Said, quoted in Bhabha, 1990:78)

Bhabha locates the stereotype in this movement between contempt and delight, which he characterises in psychoanalytic terms as a fetish. Furthermore, that dual articulation enables him to specify the rejection of difference which is at the heart of the stereotype. For a stereotype does not identify the entirely new as something 'implicated in specific historical and discursive conditions'; instead, it elides difference in favour of an otherness that is fundamentally about similarity. Consequently the body of the colonised 'other' is not perceived as different, new, strange and inexplicable, but is constituted instead in terms of the body of the coloniser—oppositionally (as abnormal, aberrant, ugly, diseased) and also, and at the same time, as sexually provocative, desirable, available and 'full of promise'.

> What is denied the colonial subject, both as colonizer and colonized, is that form of negation which gives access to the recognition of difference in the symbolic. It is that possibility of difference and circulation which would liberate the signifier of skin/culture from the signifieds of racial typology, the analytics of blood, ideologies of racial and cultural dominance or degeneration. 'Wherever he goes,' Fanon despairs, 'the negro remains a negro'—his race becomes the ineradicable sign of negative difference in colonialist discourse. For the stereotype impedes the circulation and articulation of the signifier of 'race' as anything other than its *fixity* as racism. We always already know that blacks are licentiousness, Asiatics duplicitous . . . (ibid.:80)

Bhabha notes also that these narrative representations have to be (re)produced and (re)inscribed continually in order to maintain their power, since they exist 'in the face and space of the disruption and threat from the heterogeneity of other positions':

> As a form of splitting and multiple belief, the stereotype requires, for its successful signification, a continual and repetitive chain of other stereotypes. This is the process by which the metaphoric 'masking' is inscribed on a lack which must then be concealed, that gives the stereotype both its fixity and its phantasmatic quality—the same old stories of the negro's animality, the coolie's inscrutability or the stupidity of the Irish which *must* be told (compulsively) again and afresh and is indeed differently gratifying and terrifying each time. (ibid.:81–2)

The play between 'metaphoric "masking"' and 'lack' specified here by Bhabha refers to his primary definition of the fetish as 'the simultaneous play between metaphor as substitution (making absence and difference) and metonymy (which contiguously registers the perceived lack)' (ibid.:79–80). This fundamentally conflictual co-articulation of the stereotype simultaneously recognises and denies difference. Bhabha treats it as a repetition of the primal fantasy of 'pure origin', which in psychoanalytic terms is threatened by the necessity of gendering. The double sense of the stereotype is typified in the title of Frantz Fanon's study, *Black Skin White Masks* (1967), in which Bhabha notes that 'the disavowal of difference turns the colonial subject into a misfit—a grotesque mimicry or "doubling" that threatens to split the soul and whole, undifferentiated skin of the ego' (Bhabha, 1990:80).

What makes this process so disempowering and disabling for the colonised is that it is hidden. Because the *construction* of the stereotype is concealed, the colonial subject has no way of intervening in that continual reproduction on which its efficacy depends: 'He is constructed within an apparatus of power which *contains*, in both senses of the word, an "other" knowledge—a knowledge that is arrested and fetishistic and circulates through colonial discourse as that limited form of otherness, that fixed form of difference that I have called the stereotype' (ibid.:82). As Fanon demonstrates, colonial subjects are thereby positioned to be perceived and to perceive themselves in terms of this stereotype, in so far as 'skin, as a signifier of discrimination, must be produced or processed as visible' (ibid.:83). Since the process for producing difference must be concealed so that discrimination can be officially sanctioned, it is constructed as natural: 'The difference of the object of discrimination is at once visible and natural—color as the cultural/ political sign of inferiority or degeneracy, skin as its natural "identity"' (ibid.:83). bell hooks's words on the need to unpack 'identity' and to use post-structuralist theories of subjectivity in order to unpack notions of identity and deconstruct stereotypes come to mind here. For hooks fears that the adoption of a simple kind of identity politics will result in merely another delimitation. While it may enable a limited form of solidarity, the construction of a simple or singular African-American identity could be easily naturalised as a racial stereotype, and so enter the circulation of colonialist discourse. As Bhabha explains, difference then becomes a limited fixity, colour the sign of an inferior race whose naturalised signifier is skin. In these terms, the body of the colonial subject becomes a 'natural' sign of degeneracy and inferiority.

Bhabha refines this analysis by offering reasons for that mixture of fantasy and phobia, fear and desire—noted by writers such as hooks, Said and Fanon—in the constitution of the stereotype. Bhabha relates the production of fantasy in the stereotype to a quest for 'pure origin' which informs all those institutional knowledges ('pseudo-scientific, typological, legal-administrative, eugenicist') brought to bear on the construction of the stereotype. It is therefore not simply a false image: 'It is a much more ambivalent text of projection and introjection, metaphoric and metonymic strategies, displacement, overdetermination, guilt, aggressivity; the masking and splitting of "official" and fantasmatic knowledges to construct the positionalities and oppositionalities of racist discourse' (ibid.:85).

Bhabha illustrates this point with a quotation from Fanon's *Black Skin White Masks*:

> My body was given back to me sprawled out, distorted, recolored, clad in mourning in that white winter day. The Negro is an animal, the Negro is bad, the Negro is mean, the Negro is ugly; look, a nigger, it's cold, the nigger is shivering because he is cold, the little boy is trembling because he is afraid of the nigger, the nigger is shivering with cold, that cold that goes through your bones, the handsome little boy is trembling because he thinks the nigger is quivering with rage, the little boy throws himself into his mother's arms: Mama the nigger's going to eat me up. (Fanon, quoted in ibid.:85)

In this passage Fanon reveals the dual process of fear and desire that Bhabha theorises, as well as the limitations of the stereotype: its fixity, and its devastating effect on the body of the colonised subject. As Bhabha notes, the 'little boy's' response to the 'Negro' is both an invitation and a repulsion: he invites the 'Negro' into himself in the most intimate way—to possess him, to eat him—in order to (and at the same time) reject him in those terms. And those terms are written in the fantasies (and practices) of the colonialist, since neither to be possessed nor to be eaten acknowledges the needs and desires—the reality and the difference—of the 'other'. In this process the colonised subject has his body reconstituted. (Re)inscribed by the colonialist stereotype within which he has now been subsumed, his 'sprawled out' body no longer has integrity. Fundamentally altered by its (re)production within this colonialist discourse, his body shape has become abnormal ('distorted') and his colour has been changed ('recolored') into something he does not recognise. As an 'animal' he has lost his humanity, his goodness is 'bad', his generosity 'mean', and his beauty 'ugly'. Even his bodily responses to the world around him ('shivering because he is cold') are reworked in the colonialist discourse as fear (he is perceived as 'quivering with rage'). And the contradictions of colonialist discourse are not limited to the coloniser but, as Fanon indicates, internalised also by the colonialist subject. The little ('Negro') boy who is the subject of this stereotype sees himself in these terms: his subjectivity is fundamentally altered by this encounter, and his body is both the marker and recipient of the marks of this change. The fear/desire of the coloniser is pernicious not only because it affects his own perceptions and practices, but because it is projected on to the colonised. Within colonialist discourse, the 'appropriate' response is for the colonised to experience both the fear (of his own abnormality, his essential badness, evil, meanness, ugliness) and the desire to be other (not black). As Bhabha notes, this what the stereotype reveals. The 'other' is positioned to desire a sameness, for there is no otherness in the stereotype; there is just a negative sameness, a fixity in terms that validate the colonialist. The colonised is positioned to fear and hate his own body as the marker of an 'otherness' which is not a difference but a denigration. Because the endemic ambivalence in such a positioning enacts the repetition which is necessary for the maintenance of the racist stereotype, it may be the point at which it is disrupted:

> Colonial fantasy is the continual dramatization of emergence—of difference, freedom—as the beginning of a history which is repetitively denied. Such a denial is the clearly voiced demand of colonial discourse as the legitimization of a form of rule that is facilitated by the racist fetish. (ibid.:86)

In this lies the importance of the 1960s 'Black is beautiful' movement, which aimed to reinscribe those black bodies described by racist metaphors as 'animal', 'bad', 'mean' and 'ugly' as beautiful, whole and integrated. Another example of this counter-colonialist and anti-racist disruption is a recent advertising campaign in which a beautiful indigenous Australian woman is pictured with the caption, 'They say I'm too Pretty to be Aboriginal'. The body politics of racism is complex, but it is also a point at which the stereotype (and the racist, colonialist discourse it enacts) can and must be interrogated, even though Fanon's illustration and Bhabha's careful analysis reveal not only its vulnerability but also its power.

As a Mexican-American, Richard Rodriguez writes in terms similar to Fanon's about the power of the racist stereotype to (re)inscribe the body of the marginalised social subject. He recounts his youthful sensitivity to taunts about his skin colour, and the impact on him of his parents' feelings about their (and his own) dark colouring:

> Throughout adolescence, I felt myself mysteriously marked. Nothing else about my appearance would concern me so much as the fact that my complexion was dark . . .
>
> Thirteen years old. Fourteen. In a grammar school art class, when the assignment was to draw a self-portrait, I tried and I tried but could not bring myself to shade in the face on the paper to anything like my actual tone . . .
>
> I grew divorced from my body. Insecure, overweight, listless . . . The normal, extraordinary, animal excitement of feeling my body alive—riding shirtless on a bicycle in the warm wind created by furious self-propelled motion—the sensations that first had excited in me a sense of my maleness, I denied. I was too ashamed of my body. I wanted to forget that I had a body because I had a brown body. (Rodriguez, 1990:271–2)

The racist (re)inscription of the body of the colonised subject as inferior or bad is progressively reinforced, as Rodriguez describes, by its effect on his psyche. As he becomes '[i]nsecure, overweight, listless', he loses that freedom which animates the body of the dominant social subject, and comes to hate his body as the marker of his 'otherness'. Rodriguez traces his gradual recovery from this negative constitution of his body and sense of selfhood, pointing out that he was given particular strength by the 'Black is beautiful' campaign of African-Americans. The disruption of the stereotype encapsulated in this slogan was enabling and empowering for him. In 'Black Hair/Style Politics' Kobena Mercer (1990) traces a series of such disruptions enacted in hair-styles characterised as 'black', from the conk of the 1940s through the Afro of the 1960s to the dreadlocks of the 1970s and the curly perm of the 1980s.

Mercer's analysis refers repeatedly to the opposition of 'beautiful' with 'ugly' in racist discourse:

> Classical ideologies of race established a classificatory symbolic system of color with 'black' and 'white' as signifiers of fundamental polarization of human worth—'superiority/inferiority'. Distinctions of aesthetic value, 'beautiful/ugly', have always been central to the way racism divides the world into binary oppositions in its adjudication of human worth. (Mercer, 1990:249)

For Mercer, then, the inculcation of such values is evident in the ways in which individuals (re)produce their bodies in response to such 'aestheticization'. Hair-styles are an interesting area of analysis, for while they are often represented as 'natural', in fact they never are: 'Our hair, like our skin, is a highly sensitive surface on which competing definitions of "the beautiful" are played out in struggle' (ibid.:251–2): 'We saw how the biological determinism of classical racist ideology first "politicized" our hair: its logic of devalorization of blackness radically devalued our hair, debarring it from dominant regimes of the "truth of beauty"' (ibid.:254). Mercer then demonstrates how a number of different black hair-styles have been used to challenge the dominant regime—some oppositionally (Afro and dreadlocks), some more subversively (conk). In each case, he notes, the impact of the hair-style can be appreciated only when it is contextualised by the historical conditions which give the style meaning. This is an important proviso, since otherwise the co-option of the radical style into mainstream fashion can be seen as a containment of it and therefore a failure. Mercer's point is that each style has already made its statement, has already introduced into the stereotype another of those ambivalences which Bhabha identified as its strength and weakness:

> Through aesthetic stylization each black hair-style seeks to revalorize the ethnic signifier and the political significance of each rearticulation of value and meaning depends on the historical conditions under which each style emerges.
>
> The historical significance of Afro and Dreadlocks hair-styles cannot be underestimated as marking a 'liberating' rupture or break with the dominance of white bias. (ibid.:251)

Written on the body of colonised subjects, therefore, is an explicit rejection of the stereotype which is meant to keep them enslaved and subservient. Mercer breaks with earlier interpretations (notably Malcolm X's) in not seeing the conk as a slavish reproduction of white hair-styles. Instead he argues that its combination of straightening and colouring (red) is an explicit confrontation with white norms, principally through its colour: 'Far from an attempted simulation of whiteness I think the dye was used as a stylized means of defying the "natural" color codes of conventionality in order to highlight artificiality and hence exaggerate a sense of difference' (ibid.:259). In Bhabha's terms, this tactical hair-style not only indicates the sameness inherent in the construction of the stereotype (the straightening), but in its play with conventional hair-styles (nuances of shaping and colouring) points also to a difference which the stereotype must be enacted to suppress. Mercer reads Malcolm X's revelation of his own initial pleasure in the hair-style not as a sign of degradation (as Malcolm X himself was later to do), but as an expression of his (unconscious) pleasure in its oppositional and disruptive effects, particularly when it is contextualised historically in that 'whole life-style of which the conk hair-style was a part' (ibid.:258).

> *'How it Feels to Be Coloured Me'*
> *How Does it Feel to Be White You?* (Minh-ha, 1991:66)

This analysis of the stereotype and its inscription on the bodies of the colonised returns the argument to bell hooks's essay on 'Postmodern Blackness', where she argues for the political value of post-structuralist notions of difference. For hooks, the danger of identity politics is that it may become virtually identical with the stereotypes which delimit and control the colonised in any colonialist ideology. She responds to concerns that the loss of identity politics will mean loss of solidarity and power by asserting the value of 'the authority of experience':

> An adequate response to this concern is to critique essentialism while emphasizing the significance of 'the authority of experience.' There is a radical difference between a repudiation of the idea that there is a black 'essence' and recognition of the way black identity has been specifically constituted in the experience of exile and struggle.

> When black folks critique essentialism, we are empowered to recognize multiple experiences of black identity that are the lived conditions which make diverse cultural productions possible. (hooks, 1990:29)

The experiences of Fanon and Rodriguez lend support to hooks's claim for a recognition of the role of experience in deconstructing the racism of colonialist discourse as inscribed on the body of the colonised. To value those experiences is to enable the complex constitution of black identity, which otherwise remains fixed and limited by the exigencies of the colonialist discourse in which it is conventionally produced. And as all the writers discussed above demonstrated, that is a fundamentally disruptive activity which is represented most clearly in the bodies of the colonised.

In concluding this study of the embodiment of racism—and the tactical, corporeal resistances to it—it is important to note the postscript quoted above from Trinh Minh-ha's essay, 'Outside In Inside Out' (Minh-ha, 1991). While much post-colonialist and post-structuralist writing interrogates the colonialist construction of 'otherness', little attention is paid to its consequences for colonial subjects. The white body is still too often ignored; constituted as a 'neutral' body, although nevertheless a 'correct' and 'valid' body. David Arnold (1988) demonstrates this clearly when he recounts that, while Indian train passengers were routinely, randomly and publicly examined for signs of plague, British travellers were exempted from inspection. The transparency of the white body in white colonialist discourse needs to be tackled, in order to establish not only the difference of non-white bodies, but also the 'whiteness' of those complex and multiple white bodies that are constituted by a range of historical, social, economic and political discourses. Perhaps white subjects also will then be positioned to form strategic alliances across a range of variables, including race, ethnicity, gender, age, and sexual preference.

## Bodies and ethnicities

The depredations wrought by racism and racist stereotyping on the colonised subject have made 'race' the consistent focus of arguments about colonialist discourse. The fundamental point they all make is that 'race' is a discursive category, not a biological one, although it soon becomes inscribed on the bodies of all those affected by the circulation of such discourses. 'Race', remarks Stuart Hall,

> is a *discursive* not a biological category. That is to say, it is the organizing category of those ways of speaking, systems of representation, and social practices (discourses) which utilize a loose, often unspecified set of differences in physical characteristics—skin colour, hair texture, physical and bodily features, etc.—as *symbolic markers* in order to differentiate one group socially from another. (Hall, 1992:298)

In the body politics of difference, then, race is a particularly important focus of attention. Like sex, it is a bodily marker which is readily 'naturalised' as a sign of identification or marginalisation. Yet naturalisation is always conditional on specific historical, social and economic conditions (as, for example, in the exigencies of that colonialist discourse in which both racial and racist identities are constituted). Moreover, as Stuart Hall argues in considering 'The Question of Cultural Identity' (1992), there is no such thing as racial purity. All societies are constituted by mixtures of different groups, which is the result of invasion, colonisation, and migration. 'France is [at once] Celtic, Iberic and Germanic. Germany is Germanic, Celtic and Slav. Italy is the country where . . . Gauls, Etruscans, Pelagians and Greeks, not to mention many other elements intersect in an indecipherable mixture' (Ernest Renan quoted in ibid.:298). Hall here contextualises Paul Gilroy's (1992) critique of racist pressures in the United Kingdom to 'present an imaginary definition of the nation as a unified *cultural* community' which, Gilroy argues, is a reaction to economic, social and political deterioration: 'Its dream-like construction of our sceptred isle as an ethnically purified one provides special comfort against the ravages of [national] decline' (Gilroy quoted in Hall, 1992:298). The move here from race to ethnicity is characteristic of much contemporary thought and writing on the politics of difference. After all, if race is a social and discursive construct, in what sense does it differ from ethnicity, which is conventionally described also as a social construct?

> *Ethnicity* refers to cultural practices and outlooks that distinguish a given community of people . . . Many different characteristics may serve to distinguish ethnic groups from one another, but the most usual are language, history or ancestry (real or imagined), religion, and styles of dress or adornment. Ethnic differences are *wholly learned*, a point which seems self-evident until we remember how often some such groups have been regarded as 'born to rule' or, alternatively, have been seen as 'unintelligent', innately lazy, and so forth. (Giddens, 1989:243–4)

The principal difference between this definition of ethnicity and the work on race already discussed is that the defining characteristics of ethnicity do not include physical characteristics as symbolic markers of difference. Yet it is worth noting how easily these categories are interchanged: Homi Bhabha's list of British racial stereotypes, for example, includes the Irish, who are usually regarded as ethnically rather than racially different from the British. On the one hand, this conflation of race and ethnicity draws attention to the social constructedness of both categories. On the other hand, it reinforces the fact that even characteristics which are '*wholly learned*' are inscribed bodily on those who are described by them. This unacknowledged bodily inscription perhaps provides the grounds for those more perniciously biological and genetic ascriptions (unintelligent, inherently lazy) that Giddens cites. In other words, characteristic features such as dress, adornment and religion also inscribe their users bodily. Particular religious faiths may require their followers to wear their hair in specific ways: long (Sikh), cut in a particular style (orthodox Judaism), in dreadlocks (Rastafarianism), or shaved in particular ways (as in some religious orders within Buddhism and Christianity). In each case, the wearer is bodily inscribed with a marker of her or his religion which often is also a clear indication of ethnicity. Women who wear traditional Islamic dress in western societies are equally clearly marked as 'other', whether or not their racial origins are non-western.

Analysing the resurgence of ethnicity in response to globalisation, Hall observes: 'The strengthening of local identities can be seen in the strong defensive reaction of those members of dominant ethnic groups who feel threatened by the presence of other cultures'

(Hall, 1992:308). As Hall notes, the danger in this response is basically the same as the stereotyping and negative descriptions of otherness encountered in racism. In its most extreme form, it leads to situations such as the break-up of Yugoslavia and the policy of 'ethnic-cleansing', which exemplifies Bhabha's description of the power of the drive to 'pure origins'. On the other hand, the same political, social and economic exigencies may produce new identities which can be motivated for particular political ends; Hall cites the use of the signifier 'black' in Britain in the 1970s as a point of identification for British citizens of Afro-Caribbean and Asian communities. Though each community maintained its separate cultural identity, the shared signifier 'black' enabled them to unite against their common marginalisation in the British mainstream:

> 'Black' is thus an example, not only of the *political* character of new identities—i.e. their *positional* and conjunctural character (their formation in and for specific times and places)—but also of the way identity and difference are inextricably articulated or knitted together in different identities, the one never wholly obliterating the other. (ibid.:309)

To read the bodily inscriptions of black, Pakistani British citizens is thus a complex and shifting process. While not losing their Pakistani cultural and communal identities, such citizens will also be marked in specific ways according to their participation in at least two other identities: black and British. Each gives them a decidedly different subjectivity and bodily inscription from a Pakistani subject living elsewhere. And in fact that bodily inscription will undergo further alterations, depending on the cultural context within which that subject operates (at home, at work, in relation to social institutions, and so on).

This returns us to bell hooks's analysis of racism, and the need for a notion of identity that is multiple and shifting rather than fixed and in danger of becoming stereotyped. From one point of view, only such a complex notion of identity is capable of expressing the various ways in which contemporary social subjects enact the relations of globalisation and localisation within which they are implicated. Not that this notion of cultural and ethnic complexity is new; Hall himself points out that 'ethnic purity' is a western fantasy rather than a historical fact (ibid.:305). What is new, however, is the immersion of communities in the cultural narratives of other communities and ethnicities via information technology. Although such cultural narratives are not consumed in the same way as they are by members of the indigenous cultures that produce them, foreign viewers nevertheless inscribe them bodily and psychically. This complex process allows the development of new allegiances which form new and hybrid identities, each with its corresponding bodily and psychological inscriptions.

## Race and ethnicity: degrees of 'otherness'

The body politics of ethnicity, then, is similar in many ways to the body politics of race, and often the two are directly related. However, the relationship between each of them, and their corresponding colonialist discourses, will differ according to the specific historical context. Hall notes that, as late as the nineteenth century, the Irish were treated by the English as another race. Biological and genetic analyses related the Irish directly to Africans; the ethnographer John Beddoe, using his 'Index of Nigresence', referred to the Celts of Wales and Ireland as 'Africanoid Celts' (Michie, 1992:126). This scientific means of constituting the otherness of the Irish was merely the most recent in a sequence of English revisions of Irish history, character and community, dating back at least to the sixteenth century, and necessitated by England's colonisation of Ireland. Of course, many of these attitudes persist in English society, but they are muted nowadays by changes in the political, economic and social relations between England and Ireland. 'Blackness' is now recognised as a signifier of Afro-Caribbean and some Asian communities (who themselves use it politically), but it no longer signifies the Irish. In other words, it is a mistake to think that even the most apparently 'natural' bodily characteristics (such as colour) are unchanging perceptual categories.

This is not to deny, however, the exigencies of racial and ethnic stereotypes within a particular historical and social context. For example, in Australian society this has been demonstrated by attempts to misrepresent Aboriginal features as Indian or Polynesian, in order to escape the greater prejudice and disadvantage associated with being an indigenous Australian in Australia. In her autobiography, *My Place* (1987), Sally Morgan describes her own mother's attempts to mask their family's Aboriginality as Indian. In colonialist discourse there is clearly a scale of 'otherness' for calibrating an individual's worth, and in white Australia over the last two hundred years Aboriginality has ranked very low. Each ethnic or racial stereotype, then, must be contextualised historically and discursively in order to understand its value in relation to others. The following passage from *My Place* demonstrates many of the points made in this chapter about the bodily inscription of otherness in a colonialist society, its effect on colonised subjects, the conditional nature of perceptual categories such as skin colour in the production of racist stereotypes, and the differential ways in which otherness is evaluated:

> Towards the end of the school year, I arrived home early one day to find Nan sitting at the kitchen table, crying. I froze in the doorway, I'd never seen her cry before.
>
> 'Nan . . . what's wrong?'
>
> 'Nothin'!'
>
> 'Then what are you crying for?'
>
> She lifted her arm and thumped her clenched fist hard on the kitchen table. 'You bloody kids don't want me, you want a bloody white grandmother, I'm black. Do you hear, black, black, black!' With that, Nan pushed back her chair and hurried out to her room . . .
>
> For the first time in my fifteen years, I was conscious of Nan's colouring. She was right, she wasn't white. Well, I thought logically, if she wasn't white, then neither were we. What did that make us, what did that make me? I had never thought of myself as being black before.
>
> That night, as Jill and I were lying quietly on our beds, looking at a poster of John, Paul, George and Ringo, I said, 'Jill . . . did you know Nan was black?'
>
> 'Course I did.'
>
> 'I didn't, I just found out.'
>
> 'I know you didn't. You're really dumb, sometimes. God, you reckon I'm gullible, some things you just don't see.'

'Oh . . .'

'You know we're not Indian, don't you?' Jill mumbled.

'Mum said we're Indian.'

'Look at Nan, does she look Indian?'

'I've never really thought about how she looks. Maybe she comes from some Indian tribe we don't know about.'

'Ha! That'll be the day! You know what we are, don't you?'

'No, what?'

'Boongs, we're Boongs!' I could see Jill was unhappy with the idea.

It took a few minutes before I summoned up enough courage to say, 'What's a Boong?'

'A Boong. You know, Aboriginal. God, of all things, we're Aboriginal!'

'Oh.' I suddenly understood. There was a great deal of social stigma attached to being Aboriginal at our school. (Morgan, 1987:97–8)

# 4

# Classifying Bodies: Inscriptions of Class

Sex, gender, ethnicity and race are all terms for typologies used to demarcate human bodies in specific ways in particular historical and discursive contexts. Their use inscribes individual bodies, fundamentally in terms of 'inner' and 'outer' and 'normal' and 'other'. This can result in complex positionings for a particular individual, who may be 'normal' by one criterion but 'other' according to a different one. An Anglo woman in contemporary white Australian society is both 'inner' or 'normal' (as Anglo) and 'outer' or 'other' (as female). A Koori man has a similarly complex positioning. However, these are not the only characteristics used in order to demarcate and to classify bodies in contemporary western societies. This chapter will look at another such marker, namely social class.

Because 'class' is almost invisible to the constituents of a particular classed society, it is therefore one of the most difficult markers to deal with. Accordingly, I take two (complementary) approaches here to describing and exploring the relationship between body and class. First, I give a brief account of the ways in which class has been formulated in western societies. This emphasises the fact that, from the nineteenth-century formulation of the contemporary class system, class delineation was drawn in moral, not economic, terms and that the 'moral' decisions involved were based on observations of the embodied subjectivities of working-class people. In this respect bodily inscription is endemic to the definition of class. Secondly, this class embodiment or inscription is explored through the work of French sociologist, Marcel Mauss, whose 1934 essay on 'body techniques' attempts to systematise the ways in which bodies are inscribed by their specific social positioning.

## Class(ify)ing the body

Writing about the constitution of class stereotypes in their book, *Democracy in the Kitchen* (1989), Valerie Walkerdine and Helen Lucey refer to the work of Frantz Fanon, Homi Bhabha and Audre Lord on racial stereotyping and the effects of this on the individual. Though disclaiming that racial and class stereotyping are the same mechanisms, Walkerdine and Lucey nevertheless see similarities in their operation:

> While we are not saying that the fictions and fantasies about the colonised are the same as those about the working class, we are saying that there are similar processes going on. What fantasies therefore exist of working-class women? Simultaneously as threat and desire? As promiscuous, exciting, harmful, diseased, poor mothers, yet salt of the earth, hard workers with grizzled faces and home cooking, with community spirit, warm, washerwomen with big arms, big breasts, big hearts. (Walkerdine and Lucy, 1989:39)

This statement raises a number of points at issue in the constitution of that discursive formation known as the 'working class'. First, it notes that a process of stereotyping (similar to the one discussed by Bhabha, hooks and others) is involved in constituting class identities, and that it constitutes the working class in the position of 'other'. As a corollary, it questions the particular fantasies which fetishise the stereotype in the case of working-class women. Secondly, it offers a set of terms by which working-class women are constituted discursively. Almost all those terms are connected in some way with sexuality, and specifically with either illicit sex or maternity. On the one hand, working-class women are somehow sexually deviant, and therefore both exciting and a potential source of corruption, both moral and physical. On the other hand, they are elementally maternal figures, synonymous with comfort, generosity, caring and selflessness. In both cases the women are described predominantly in physical terms as particular kinds of bodies which can be used and exploited, but which can also comfort and nurture. This description recalls Lynette Finch's study of the constitution of the working class as a discursive formation in *The Classing Gaze* (1993).

Finch argues that originally the working class was constituted not in political or economic terms, but through the moralistic observations of nineteenth-century middle-class 'social explorers':

> The range of concerns through which middle class observers made sense of the behaviour of the observed, included references to: living conditions (in particular how many people lived in a single room); drinking behaviour (both male and female); language (including both the types of things that were spoken about, and the manner in which they were referred to—literally the types of words used); and children's behaviour (specifically how closely they were watched and controlled, and the types of things they were allowed to talk about). These were *moral*, not economic, references. (Finch, 1993:10)

Throughout the nineteenth century, therefore, the working classes were systematically constituted, judged and evaluated by fundamentally moral criteria. In Finch's terms, they were divided into two groups: the respectable working class and the non-respectable. By the end of the nineteenth century, however, a new method of surveillance had evolved:

> At the end of the nineteenth century a new way of observing and making sense of the world allowed a different set of evidence to be accepted, even if it was not visible. This psychological style of reasoning sought out new presences, devised ways of understanding knowledge through the measuring of an invisible concept, intelligence, and understood the drives of humans through a new invisible force, sexuality.
>
> Sexuality replaced morality as the primary grid through which knowledge about society in general, but working class behaviour in particular, was organised and acted upon. (ibid.:13)

In their analysis of contemporary attitudes to the working class, and specifically to working-class women, Walkerdine and Lucey detect this same principle in operation. For Finch, the constitution within bourgeois discourse of the working class (and by implication the middle class—since the working class is the defining 'other' of the middle class in bourgeois discourse), is linked inextricably with the discourse of sexuality:

> Within psychological reasoning it was the late nineteenth century construction of sexuality which provided the grid through which individuals were fixed within 'their' class category. Had the discourse of sexuality not emerged at this time, the working class as a distinct knowable entity would have emerged as a fundamentally different construct. Conversely, had the working classes not already been articulated as sites for middle class scrutiny and intervention, sexuality would have emerged in relation to a different discursive order. The discourses of sexuality and of the working class were deployed together, each one feeding the other, each overlapping and interrelating. (ibid.:147)

Finch notes that the vocabulary of sexuality replaced that of 'the flesh', a Christian moral construct that signified specific acts rather than the propensities of specific bodies. In the language of 'the flesh', for example, sodomy was a particular kind of sexual activity which was illegal. By the end of the nineteenth century, however, when the language of sexuality came to dominate, sodomy was no longer a particular (and illegal) activity, but the (unnatural and illegal) activity of a particular kind of person, a male homosexual. 'Within a history of sexuality', Finch observes, 'what is important is not the lawful and the unlawful, but rather the natural and the unnatural' (ibid.:39). Once the working class was constituted (sexually) as a particular formation, working-class individuals were bodily inscribed with the marks of that formation.

The next section will deal with the implications of this process before considering the inscription of class which has developed from the work of Marcel Mauss on the 'techniques of the body' (Mauss, 1992:461). Mauss argues that the activities and behaviours which constitute the everyday reality of a person are inscribed bodily. Perhaps this notion can be used also to explore the differences that demarcate one class from another.

## Sexuality: class and/of the body

The work of Walkerdine and Lucey raises the issue of the sexualisation of working-class women, and how this is used to constitute those women discursively. Effectively, they are reduced to particular kinds of bodies: sexually provocative and dangerous, or maternal and nurturing. In each case the (female) body is the primary marker of social class. Differences in the ascription correspond to Finch's account of the splitting of the working class by middle-class observers into respectable and non-respectable components. Even when the grounds of the description were moral, however, the disposition of the body—crowded together with other bodies, inebriated or sober, speaking scatologically or not, disciplining children or not—was a central concern. The method by which this social taxonomy was accomplished—middle-class observation—was doubtless largely responsible for the fetishisation of the body. Those observers did not engage sufficiently with the everyday lives of their subjects of study to understand their motivations and behaviours, or the narratives they constructed about how they lived (that is, their culture). It is not surprising, therefore, that their ('scientific') observations could report only on bodily disposition, and then only from a largely uncomprehending other (middle-class) perspective. Carolyn Steedman makes this point in *Landscape for a Good Woman* (1986), when she discusses the inability of the social observer, Henry Mayhew, to understand the account of her life given to him by a nine-year-old watercress seller. Mayhew was unable to make sense of the girl's story because he could not align it with his own (middle-class) preconceptions about childhood—a kind of childhood that this girl (because of her class) had never known.

When middle-class observation is expressed in sexual rather than moral terms, the fetishisation of the body is equally prominent but construed differently. Since the middle classes are also implicated in the discourse of sexuality—it is, after all, a 'natural' attribute—the body becomes a source of possible, if dangerous alliance between the two classes. For Walkerdine and Lucey, as well as for Steedman, this nexus is the crucial factor in middle-class treatments of working-class women. As bodies to be exploited, working-class women are a potential source of bodily pleasure, but they are also a danger for middle-class men, and, by extension, middle-class women. On the one hand, it is feared that working-class women will use their bodies (the promise of bodily pleasure) to entrap middle-class men into marriage, or at least financial support. Because that may well compromise the marriages or marriage-prospects of middle-class men, it also challenges the position of middle-class women. On the other hand, as common sources of (illicit, but not unnatural or illegal) pleasure for middle-class men, working-class women are potential breeding-grounds for disease, which will not only (re)infect the men, but may be taken home to their middle-class spouses. Steedman discusses this (middle-class) perception as part of a bourgeois myth about working-class women, which she terms the 'goose-girls may marry kings' story (Steedman, 1986:15–6). According to this myth, working-class women will exploit their bodies in order to gain not just economic but also social advantage. Goose girls get more than just the economic support of kings; they marry them—and so gain social and political power and status. This possibility is enormously threatening, of course, for both middle-class men and women, suggesting as it does that the boundary between the classes can be transgressed. It is also a problem in the relationship between working-class men and women, since it constructs working-class women as potentially 'class traitors', who are liable to abandon their culture and change their class allegiances at the prospect of greater economic advantage.

All of these readings of working-class women recur in fiction—in romantic tales of servant girls who marry their masters (as in Regency romance); in detective fiction, where a female villain is often the source of social disease (Cawelti, 1976:156); deconstructed by Thomas Hardy in *Tess of the D'Urbervilles* (1891); and evident in many filmic and televisual portrayals of 'common' women (working-class mistresses) whom men leave for women of 'quality' (either middle-class women or 'respectable' working-class women). As Walkerdine and Lucey note, this recalls racial and ethnic stereotyping, featuring as it does the same mixture of fear and desire as pleasure is linked to bodily and social disease. One might note also bell hooks's account of the social challenge offered by interracial love, which resulted in the incarceration of white men in mental institutions to protect them from their apparent sexual and social abnormality (hooks, 1990:58).

Similarly stereotyped is the upper class or aristocracy. Finch notes that 'two classes—the upper class or aristocracy and the non-respectable working class—were sites of tension within the ordered representation [of bourgeois society]' (Finch, 1993:146). Toward the end of the nineteenth century, there were numerous fictional accounts of the diseased and decadent upper class, that 'other' class which had to be accounted for in middle-class (re)constructions of society. This persistent stereotype perhaps accounts in part for the fascination with royal families (actual and metaphorical). Again they are imbued with a mixture of fear and desire, loathing and fascination, as their status and privilege are contextualised in their sexual exploits. One of the striking fictional examples of this stereotype is the vampire, particularly Bram Stoker's Dracula, who is both upper class and non-Anglo. Invading respectable bourgeois London from the depths of feudal Transylvania, Dracula was notable not only for his foreignness—signified by his stilted English—but also for the aristocratic arrogance with which he treats his middle-class pursuers: '"You think to baffle me, you—with your pale faces all in a row, like sheep in a butcher's . . . Your girls that you all love are mine already; and through them you and others shall yet be mine—my creatures, to do my bidding and to be my jackals when I want to feed. Bah!"' (Stoker, 1983:306). Dracula sweeps into England like a horde of plague-carrying rats and attempts to infect bourgeois society by penetrating the bodies of middle-class women, a displaced reference to sexual intercourse (Cranny-Francis, 1988, 1990a, 1990b). The rat-like teeth of the Nosferatu, a version of the vampire, are another reference to the vampire's plague-like nature and actions; the Murnau film, *Nosferatu* (F. W. Murnau, 1921) explicitly associates the vampire with the plague-carrying rats. Disease, then, and particularly sexually transmitted disease, is a metaphorical expression of that mixture of fear and desire aroused when the boundaries that separate the classes are acknowledged to be porous. For the middle class, the principal carriers of this disturbing disease were working-class women and the aristocracy. Hardy's description of Angel Clare's class-based rejection of Tess in *Tess of the D'Urbervilles* epitomises these bourgeois obsessions: 'Decrepit families imply decrepit wills, decrepit conduct. Heaven, why did you [Tess] give me a handle for despising you more by informing me of your descent! Here was I thinking you a new-sprung child of nature; there were you, the belated seedling of an effete aristocracy' (Hardy, 1978:302). Hardy's Clare summarises middle-class responses to both working-class women and the aristocracy, which establish them as the 'other' of middle-class respectability.

This aspect of the stereotype—the sexual predator or prey—corresponds to Finch's 'non-respectable' working class, made up of those condemned as drunkards and child abusers in middle-class regulation of the working classes (Finch, 1993). The 'respectable' working class, on the other hand, is typified by the other side of Walkerdine and Lucey's portrayal of the middle-class stereotype of the working-class woman: the motherly, nurturing woman—with 'big arms, [and] big breasts'—whose body is inscribed by this role (Walkerdine and Lucey, 1989:39). This working-class woman constitutes no threat, for her (now) unfashionably maternal body signifies nurturing, caring and even servitude. She, too, is paralleled in ethnic and racial stereotypes by the woman whose chief value is her labour power, particularly when harnessed to the bodily demands of the middle class. In her case, however, the demands she meets are for hygiene, the preparation and serving of food, child-care and house-cleaning. Her association with the middle class is again intimate, but not sexual. She is a labouring body. Although her emotional warmth (signified by her 'big heart') is part of her value, her needs and desires are not consulted. In many ways she resembles the caring and compassionate female slave of early Anglo-American fiction. Both aspects of the stereotype of the working-class woman fetishise the physical, the bodily. She is perceived not as a subject who has been socialised and acculturated differently, but as a specific kind of body—seductive or motherly—to be regulated and exploited in specific ways.

Stereotypical images of working-class men similarly elide the specificities of working-class culture and life, and are based on observations of their behaviour and practices by middle-class men. The characteristics by which working-class men were described and evaluated in the nineteenth century were the same as those for working-class women: sobriety, living conditions, language and children's behaviour. Again, both the description and the evaluation were primarily moral, not economic, and based on the reading of that bodily inscription by middle-class observers. They judged what they *saw*, and that judgement was made through the lens of a different (middle-class) culture.

One important consequence of this mode of analysis is that working-class men were similarly constituted as particular kinds of bodies, who drank or were sober, lived in crowded conditions, used particular kinds of language, and treated children in particular ways. In western terms, as discussed in chapters 1 and 2, masculinity is associated with 'mind' and not 'body', which in turn is the preserve of women, of femininity. Politically and socially, however, the description of working-class men in terms of 'body' established the dominance and priority of middle-class men, who reserved for themselves the symbolic status of 'mind'. Bodily, working-class males were men, but politically and socially they were denied the kudos associated with masculinity. Clearly, the mind/body split was in this case not only gendered but also class-bound.

The shift in the evaluative terms from nineteenth-century moralism to twentieth-century sexuality did not alter this perception of working-class men. In both periods, however, it was conceded that working-class men behave somewhat differently from working-class women, and notably in their potential for violence. The violence of working-class men was thought to be produced by a propensity to dominate (as an expression of their masculinity), combined with their primarily physical nature (as delineated by middle-class men). By contrast, middle-class men were thought more able to control (by mental effort) any violent impulses they may have. Again, as in the stereotyping of the racial and ethnic 'other', we witness the operation of displacement. In those stereotypes, it will be recalled, oppression is displaced as fear and exploitation as desire. In this instance, however, the violent oppression of working-class men by the middle classes (in unsafe working conditions, brutally long working hours, and violent suppression of union activities) is displaced and reconstituted as a 'brutal' feature of 'violent' working-class men.

Finch notes that this violence was established as a characteristic of (male) working-class life through observations of working-class living conditions. She reports a number of legal cases in which overcrowding was held directly responsible for acts of incest, committed predominantly by fathers on daughters. Since such conditions were also considered a defining characteristic of working-class life, working-class men were thereby constituted as having a potential for sexual violence by 'nature' (where 'nature' means a propensity of character produced by specific living conditions). And again, it is not difficult to see this as a displacement of middle-class male behaviour, the implication being that incest did not happen in middle-class families because everyone had a separate bed.

Although potentially violent, working-class men are also seen as more physically competent and more at ease with their bodies. This combination provides another titillating stereotype, not unlike the image of the black man as a 'peripatetic phallus': this is the working-class lover, the 'bit of rough' for the use of middle-class women and men. In terms of sexual prowess, working-class men are commonly depicted as more elemental and physically more confident than middle-class men. A range of images derives from this stereotype, including most notably Mellors, the gamekeeper of D. H. Lawrence's novel, *Lady Chatterley's Lover* (1928), and more recently Baines, the seaman in the film, *The Piano* (1993). While their physical strength and power (and their directness about sexuality) are a source of desire for the supposedly repressed middle class, the potential violence with which they are also associated adds a piquancy which produces that stereotypical combination of fear and desire.

Despite their supposed potential for violence, however, these male working-class characters are not as disturbing as their female counterparts. The reason for this may be twofold. First, a working-class man is unlikely to perpetrate violence against a middle-class lover, since in class terms he is highly disadvantaged in such an encounter. Secondly, working-class men pose less of a threat to bourgeois society than working-class women because any children by such liaisons are, in middle-class terms, characterised by the class of the father, and as such do not intrude into the middle class. Of course, the paternity of those children may be hidden by their mother, in which case the threat is still potentially there. Nevertheless, working-class women offer a much more substantial threat, because any children they might have by middle-class men are legally entitled to the support of their fathers. This is certainly an incursion into middle-class life. For this reason, the sexuality of working-class women attracts a particularly vicious stereotypical projection; it is a disease that aligns them with that other class which threatens middle-class dominance, the upper class.

So working-class men are commonly portrayed as sexually competent and promiscuous, but also as exploitable and expendable. This construction of them as sexual bodies for middle-class consumption is common in a wide range of fictional and other material. The constitution of the rock star, Bruce Springsteen, as a sex object was based on this stereotype, particularly in the videoclip of 'Dancing in the Dark' and its parodic counterpart, 'I'm On Fire'. The working-class men of soap operas (like Jake of *Melrose Place*) frequently fill this role; and in the film *The Piano*, George Baines is clearly constituted as the bodily 'other' of the repressed and physically incompetent Stewart. Although Baines wins the woman, this is a victory won at considerable personal expense to her (since she loses a finger), and is complicated by racial stereotypes. In each case the working-class male characters are represented as both desirable and to some extent dangerous, but not as diseased, deceitful or harmful. In fact here, as in many stories of working-class male lovers, the cuckolded middle-class male partner is shown subsequently as the more violent, and to exercise that violence against the woman.

A corollary of this construction of working-class men as 'body' is that they are represented frequently as more caring and nurturing than middle-class men. Their constitution as loving fathers capable of caring for children in physically and emotionally tender ways is the positive side of this stereotyping. A popular Australian example is D'Arcy Niland's *The Shiralee* (1957). By contrast middle-class men appear frigid and authoritarian. In Finch's terms, this is the embodied expression of the 'respectable' working-class man, who, while still described in primarily physical terms, exemplifies the positive features of that description.

It is worth noting at this stage that working-class women and men offer bodily resistances—which draw on the very terms which motivate the stereotype—to middle-class scrutiny and regulation. For working-class men, bodily prowess—as sportsmen, for example—is sometimes a tactically useful way of deflecting middle-class condescension. For working-class women the situation is more complex, since it involves a doubling of their positioning as 'other'. Nevertheless, the mothering skills of working-class women might be a means of deflecting unwelcome intrusions from the middle class. In neither case, however, are the culture and voice of working-class people heard. Instead the dominant voice is that of middle-class culture, which never falters more than momentarily in its ongoing and continual reconstruction both of itself and 'others'. Although in classed societies the class differences between individuals are often said to be invisible, it is obvious that in practice they are clearly perceived by those involved in any particular situation.

It is clear that this middle-class construction of working-class men and women in terms of the 'body' is not only partial, but also politically and socially motivated. How, then, is it made to seem 'natural'? As noted earlier, it is not uncommon for members of a class-structured society to deny that class is a visible feature or attribute of particular individuals. Sex, race and ethnicity, it is claimed, are physically and bodily apparent in features such as secondary sexual characteristics and skin colour (however contingent such descriptions might be). By contrast, it is said to be often very difficult to tell the differences between members of different social classes simply by looking at them. The next section of this chapter argues against the notion of class invisibility, which fails to account for the material construction and inscription of individual bodies by the classed society in which they live and work. Perhaps the ultimate denial of the class-based nature of a society is when its class differences are naturalised so effectively that they seem invisible. Yet for such a society to operate within its own (class-based) boundaries, those differences must nevertheless be apparent to each of its members at any time.

## Body techniques: classing the body

In order to describe these 'invisible' differences some recent theorists have turned to the work of Marcel Mauss, and especially to his

1934 article on 'Techniques of the Body'. This establishes a framework for rethinking conceptualisations of 'the body' and the ways in which it is inscribed by everyday life to become the body of a particular person. Mauss's basic premise is that there is no 'natural' way of performing any action, even something as basic as walking, as was shown in his observations of the walking gait of Maori women:

> This was an acquired, not a natural way of walking. To sum up, there is perhaps no 'natural way' for the adult. A fortiori when other technical facts intervene: to take ourselves, the fact that we wear shoes to walk transforms the positions of our feet: we certainly feel it when we walk without them. (Mauss, 1992:460)

Prior to this example Mauss recalls the arrival in France of American fashions of walking:

> American walking fashions had begun to arrive over here, thanks to the movies. This was an idea I could generalize. The positions of the arms and hands while walking form a social idiosyncrasy—they are not simply a product of some purely individual, almost completely psychic, arrangements and mechanisms. (ibid.:458)

With this in mind Mauss claims he can recognise a girl who has been raised in a convent by the way she holds her fists closed when walking. This apparently individual trait can be located, he believes, in a specific kind of socialisation. And after recalling being told as a young boy at school not to walk with his hands loose, he concludes: 'Thus, there exists an education in walking, too' (ibid.). Mauss effectively rejects the notion that there is a primary guiding psyche or soul, which the body interprets or represents in idiosyncratic ways. Instead he argues that individual bodies are formed and inscribed by the educational activities of everyday life, which include class, ethnic, racial, gendered and sexed experiences: 'The body is man's first and most natural instrument. Or more accurately, not to speak of instruments, man's first and most natural technical object, and at the same time his first technical means, is his body' (ibid.:461). Instead of an instrumental conception of the body, Mauss proposes a 'psychosociological taxonomy' (ibid.:462) to describe the inscriptions of the body by the everyday. He mentions in particular how techniques of the body are divided by sex and by age (ibid.:462–4). However, it may also be possible to discuss differences of class in terms of this reconceptualisation of the body.

As we have seen, Walkerdine and Lucey link stereotypes of working-class women with the regulatory practices of bourgeois society. Those stereotypes are essentially embodied characterisations: the 'big arms, big breasts' image represents a particular bodily inscription, namely of a non-bourgeois woman engaged in manual labour and with a large number of children. Extending Mauss's taxonomy, such stereotypes might be conceptualised as 'physio-psycho-sociological assemblages', which characterise an individual life by its social positioning in a particular class culture. The example is simplistic, of course, for the working-class woman inscribed in this way will also manifest her social class in her dress, adornment, manner, posture, walking, speaking, interactions with others, ways of eating and sleeping, and so on. A cultural analysis of her life will not fetishise her body to the degree that the middle-class stereotype did. Nevertheless, her body will be seen as marked by her participation in that particular culture in which she has learned how to eat and walk, speak and sleep, dress and stand. Even when simply standing still, her posture, attitude and manner all communicate meanings that signify a particular class.

Such coding of class behaviours is nowhere more evident than in encounters between members of different classes. Here it is important to avoid the reductive stereotyping of class inscription on to the bodies of particular individuals. Nevertheless, if we accept that class is among those experiences that inscribe themselves bodily, then we must accept the possibility that these embodied attitudes and behaviours can be described and analysed. It may be useful, therefore, to consider a number of sites at which conjunctions of class occur.

In *Fashioning the Feminine* (1991), Pam Gilbert and Sandra Taylor discuss the ways in which teenage girls construct gendered identities for themselves from a range of materials, including television programmes, magazines and novels. They report how such interactions (like the classrooms in which they spend so much of their time) function as sites of contestation, in which girls differentiate between particular kinds of identities, and formulate and embody identities for themselves. This is not to say that such contests are performed by subjects who are completely self-aware, knowing and integrated; but then, no contest ever is. Among the identities that girls embody in this process is a class identity, which is constituted by interactions between their home class culture, the cultures of the school and other extra-domestic institutions, and their own socially and politically motivated choices. Like Patricia Gillard (1986), Gilbert and Taylor have also identified the ways in which teenage girls use television viewing, for example, to examine the choices available for women in the workplace. Gillard found that the televisual representation of a successful professional woman was used by some girls as a role-model, inspiring them to move beyond conservative career stereotypes which are often class-motivated. Inspired by such a character, a working-class girl engages in a trajectory which may be counter to her class expectations. How this complex class contestation is experienced and embodied is the subject of Willy Russell's play and screenplay, *Educating Rita* (1985).

Here the main character undertakes exactly this kind of trajectory. Beginning as a full-time hairdresser who undertakes part-time university study, she then becomes a full-time student and part-time waiter before finally graduating with the potential to enter the professional work-force. In the movie, Rita's transformations are signified most clearly by her changing embodiment. It should be noted here that some working-class women have found the portrayal of Rita (particularly at the beginning of the film) offensive, mainly because the working-class subjectivity she embodied is seen through middle-class eyes. Nevertheless, from another viewpoint, this is what makes the film so important and interesting, for it reveals not only different class specificities, but also the ways in which they are seen by members of different classes.

At the beginning of the movie Rita is shown entering the university grounds; she is clearly out of place, as her dress, presentation, posture, gait and manner suggest. The fact that the film-makers are able to indicate Rita's class background by such features before the audience knows anything about her proves that socially encoded class differences are clearly visible as embodied characteristics. It may be argued, of course, that such characteristics are overdetermined in these early scenes. Rita has a frizzy perm and her hair is peroxide blonde; she wears a very tight, short skirt and her clothes are not 'put together' in a middle-class way; she also walks very awkwardly, tripping up in her high heels as she attempts to negotiate the cobbled courtyard of the university. As some working-class viewers note, Rita is here a virtual caricature of working-class femininity, as read through middle-class perceptions. Rita's mannerisms too are derived from working-class culture, but they are all concentrated in one individual who is then placed in an institutional setting which is hostile to her. She appears funny, awkward, laughable. Indeed, the film deliberately sets up such an initial response to Rita in order to educate its audience about their own class-based prejudices.

As the film proceeds and Rita's lifestyle changes, so too do her manner, dress, body language and accent. At varying stages she comes to embody the working-class woman, the enthusiastic student, the student member of a 'fashionable' (that is, wealthy, middle-class) crowd, and finally the graduate. In the process Rita moves from the working-class culture of her home (her husband and parents) to that hybrid culture (working-class and middle-class) she constructs when she leaves her husband; she then experiences the predominantly middle-class culture of her fashionable friends before settling finally into a more self-consciously hybrid culture that she lives in at the end of the film. At each stage her class culture is clearly evident in her dress and manner. In fact, Rita's sometimes unsuccessful (because awkward and forced) attempts to embody another (middle-class) lifestyle are used to comment on the clash of cultures she experiences. Her final position on this matter is that she will consider what each culture has to offer her and choose (as much as any individual is ever free to) what she will make of her life. This very optimistic conclusion elides, of course, the difficulties faced by people living outside the class culture in which they were raised. But it also makes the point that individuals often experience a range of different class behaviours, each of which contributes in specific ways to their own idiosyncratic embodiment of class (and other) positionings. In so doing, *Educating Rita* explicitly argues against an essentialist notion of class as something unchangeable. At the same time it acknowledges that bodily markers of class do indeed exist and, perhaps even more importantly, that they are interpreted differently by observers from different classes.

The other principal character in *Educating Rita* is Rita's university tutor, Frank. Frank is a cynical, alcoholic and self-indulgent man who is intrigued by what he perceives as Rita's freshness. When she later adopts the dress and many of the mannerisms of his other middle-class students, Frank is horrified, feeling he has betrayed what was 'special' in Rita. Again, all these perceptions and conclusions are seen through middle-class eyes. As Rita later points out to Frank, what he interpreted as 'freshness' was her class difference, which he did not find threatening because he is positioned socially in a dominant role to her: he knows what Rita has come to learn.

Later, as Frank sees Rita begin to change, she is no longer the tame working-class person—the alien—he can patronise. Rita senses in Frank's earliest perceptions of her a recognition of difference which is also a description of 'otherness'. She makes this very clear to him when she reveals the great stress his early invitation to dinner has caused her. In the film, Rita is shown changing from one outfit to another, being dissatisfied with them all, and finally deciding not to attend the party. It is a measure of Frank's class blindness that he has no understanding either of the problems that his invitation causes not only her but also her husband Denny, or that in such a situation Rita would be a curiosity exploited and humiliated by his friends. He sees her difference merely as an otherness which piques his curiosity, while leaving him firmly in control. As Rita tries on her different outfits, the viewer is positioned to see them as tacky and tasteless (again no doubt by a filmic overdetermination of these costumes and the actor's wearing of them). Rita is being judged in middle-class terms, but what this demonstrates is both the alienness of her culture and the limitations of the value judgements that accompany middle-class perceptions. This is, after all, where the problem lies. It is not that the terms of the perception are different. It is rather that the difference is unacknowledged, and therefore becomes the basis of a series of value judgements.

There are marked differences between working-class and middle-class cultures, and the usual way of evaluating them is to equate working-class with lack of taste, and middle-class with taste. 'Taste' is therefore an extremely important term in the delineation and maintenance of not so much class cultures as class division, that is, class conflict (see Bernstein, 1975:151–6; Bourdieu, 1984). This judgement of taste is not consequent upon particular behaviours, but is motivated initially by the mere self-presentation of the embodied subject. Nothing need be said or done: class-based judgements can be made entirely on appearances. Carolyn Steedman's repudiation of the 'goose-girls may marry kings' narrative in *Landscape for a Good Woman* is motivated by her understanding of such class-based evaluations. That narrative elides the class differences which would tell a king very early on what kind of attention he needs to bestow on the goose-girl. Conversely, without a thorough knowledge of cultures other than her own, no goose-girl would know how to present herself to a king (Steedman, 1986; Cranny-Francis, 1990b). This narrative enacts that middle-class complex of fear and desire which constitutes a stereotype of working-class femininity: the beautiful working-class woman who uses her physical attributes to elevate herself economically and socially. Class difference is again elided so that class identity can be naturalised.

Steedman, Walkerdine and others draw attention to the pernicious influence of class-based judgements on individuals from different class backgrounds. They are particularly damaging to working-class people, who may be excluded from jobs, from gaining credit in a range of different institutional settings, and from receiving a sympathetic hearing from (middle-class) authorities because they seem neither credible nor competent. These judgements—of credibility, belonging, and competence—may be based primarily on bodily inscriptions of class difference, which middle-class people making the judgements subsequently evaluate as inadequacy, inferiority or lack. Once again the problem is that the basis of such judgements—class difference—is elided, so that instead of being recognised *as* judgements they are seen as 'natural' responses to particular individuals.

Marcel Mauss's work is important because it begins to develop a framework for examining embodiment or bodily inscription in ways which acknowledge difference instead of devaluing otherness. Mauss uses the term *habitus* (more recently identified with the work of the French sociologist, Pierre Bourdieu) to describe that complex of activities and behaviours which characterises the lived experience of individuals. Mauss defines *habitus* this way:

> These 'habits' do not vary just with individuals and their imitations; they vary especially between societies, educations, proprieties and fashions, types of prestige. In them, we should see the techniques and work of collective and individual practical reason rather than, in the ordinary way, merely the soul and its repetitive faculties. (Mauss, 1992:458)

The individual *habitus* results from an idiosyncratic inflection of a range of shared positionings. Bourdieu writes similarly in *Homo Academicus*: '*Habitus* is a system of shared social dispositions and cognitive structures which generates perceptions, appreciations and actions' (Bourdieu, 1988:279). In *Distinction* Bourdieu notes:

> The habitus is necessarily internalized and converted into a disposition that generates meaningful practices and meaning-giving perceptions; it is a general, transposable disposition which carries out a systematic, universal application—beyond the limits of what has been directly learnt—of the necessity inherent in the learning conditions. That is why an agent's whole set of practices (or those of a whole set of agents produced by similar conditions) are both systematic, inasmuch as they are the product of the application of identical (or interchangeable) schemes, and systematically distinct from the practices constituting another life-style. (Bourdieu, 1984:170)

While Bourdieu's analysis of taste in *Distinction* (1984) has been criticised on a number of grounds (Frow, 1990), its power and importance lie in the attempt to denaturalise class-based and class-motivated judgements, and to see their function instead as the maintenance of class boundaries. As Bourdieu's definitions of *habitus* acknowledge, individuals do not act in ways which are wholly idiosyncratic; instead, they enact (idiosyncratically) the attitudes and values, behaviours and practices that their background and training, home and institutional cultures teach them. Mauss's early work on the body is an important supplement to this kind of enquiry, since it provides the beginnings of a framework for the analysis of class difference (as manifest in judgements of taste) at the level of embodiment, of bodily inscription. Without such a framework, the analysis of class difference is too easily naturalised as individual difference. When class difference is constituted as a judgement of taste, the victims almost inevitably are the socially disadvantaged. Exceptions occur only when a particular individual is satirised as lacking in taste, or when the upper class as a whole is satirised for its eccentric (that is, non-bourgeois) tastes.

This is an important area for research and analysis. The main aim is to make visible those 'invisible' markers of class that constitute western society. The questions generated in this field are many and various. For example, how do we discuss the portrayal of working-class characters by middle-class actors? Can we simply assume that a middle-class actor such as James Dean, who often portrayed working-class men in films, understood working-class masculinity so thoroughly and internalised working-class culture so completely, that what we see on the screen is a true image of working-class masculinity? Or did his portrayals constitute a complex reworking of working-class masculinity through internalised middle-class perceptions that render stereotypical or hybrid the working-class characters he acted? Conversely, how does the working-class background of an actor such as Michael Caine impinge on his portrayal of middle-class characters? Do we encounter here another hybrid—this time the embodiment of a middle-class subjectivity seen through the eyes of a working-class man? To what extent do the demands of audiences and of film-makers intervene to heighten or modify the resultant hybrid and/or stereotypical construction of class identity?

These questions are related to an earlier point about the complex lived experience of many individuals who bridge different cultures in their domestic and working life. How is that process performed bodily? What hostilities or misunderstandings do they suffer because of (mis)readings of their embodied and hybrid subjectivities?

It might be argued that in western societies the semiotics of class is as elusive and transparent as the semiotics of music. For a long time the only available means of studying and analysing music were historical and ethnographic. Music, it was claimed, is linked directly to the emotions, and cannot be constrained within 'reductive' interpretive frames. As Theo van Leeuwen claims, the effect of this attitude is to mystify music as an unknowable and unpredictable system. Transparency and naturalisation (music = emotion) simultaneously confirm the power of music as a semiotic, to be protected (as it therefore is) from analysis and critique (van Leeuwen, 1988).

Embodiments of class may well constitute a similarly transparent and powerful system of meanings. Unable to be named without deconstructing and thus destroying the operations of middle-class ideology, 'techniques of the body' constitute a powerful system of identity maintenance and control. What they maintain is not the specific nature of embodied working-class or middle-class or upper-class subjectivities—all of which are fluid and flexible—but the *boundaries* between these positionings, which particular individuals may traverse repeatedly in the course of their everyday lives.

To delineate the embodied characteristics of class is a difficult and politically risky practice, as the sociologist Basil Bernstein discovered when he was effectively silenced (by bitter and continual critique) after describing differences between middle-class and working-class uses of language. Furthermore, given the fluid nature of such identities, the construction and application of definitive frames of interpretation are likely to be not only misleading but also catalytic in the production of different readings and positionings. For example, a class-specific frame may be read by a member either of that class or of a different class and then deliberately subverted (in so far as that is possible) in an embodiment of her or his own. In this way, the interpretive frames would themselves become part of the continuing evolution of classed embodiments, rather than definitive of one particular embodiment. Typical of this process is the production of embodied female subjectivities in women's magazines. Although these constructions are inevitably classed, they are used transparently by women of different classes to regulate their own embodiments. This does not mean that women slavishly reproduce these inscriptions. But they are a major site of contestation with respect to class as well as gender, and are doubtless influential in the continuing evolution of classed embodiments.

These reservations aside, it is nevertheless crucially important to recognise that the classed embodiments of western societies not only exist but function to maintain their (changing) class structures. The reason why this is important is that so many decisions about people's lives are based on conscious or unconscious perceptions of their class identity and difference. And as I have argued, this perception is not recognised for what it is—namely an articulation of similarity or difference—but is (re)interpreted and naturalised in middle-class ideology as a matter of taste. To understand class embodiments we need a couple of perspectives, one provided by the historical constitution of class identity, and the other by a material analysis of how the embodied subject—as an experiential and semiotic formation—must be recognised not as some idiosyncratic manifestation of an individual identity, but as a complex expression of social positionings, including those of class.

5

# Cyborgs and Wet-ware: Technologised Bodies

One of the most popular subjects of recent writing about the body is the effect of technology on twentieth-century understandings of the 'human' body. Here the key questions concern the nature, and future, of the body in a time of such rapidly developing and expanding technologies as infotech (information technology), biological engineering, and robotics. Of course, this metaphysical (but also highly political) exploration of the human body intersects crucially with issues of gender, race, ethnic and class identity. One such instance—the development of reproductive technologies and their implications for the constitution and maintenance of gender identities—was discussed in Chapter 2. This chapter will focus on interrogations of the nature of the 'human', which go back at least as far as the development of modern industrial technology in the early nineteenth century.

At that time one of the earliest fictional explorations of this question was Mary Shelley's *Frankenstein* (1818), discussed already in relation to reproductive technologies. Shelley's investigations have many contemporary successors, such as Philip K. Dick's novel, *Do Androids Dream of Electric Sheep?* (1969), and its film version, *Blade Runner* (Ridley Scott, 1982), as well as the James Cameron films, *The Terminator* (1984) and *Terminator 2: Judgment Day* (1990). Some of these fictions will be considered here, together with the philosophical and political debates that motivate and sustain them. These debates will be placed also in relation to changing conceptualisations of the body prompted by the nature of contemporary information technologies. A reference will be made to the development of new hybrid fictional genres, whose primary motivation is to explore this nexus between the body and technology.

## Cyborgs: machine-men and the man-made body

Explorations of the relationship between the human body and technology originate with the development of modern industrial technology in the late eighteenth and early nineteenth centuries. Although there are antecedents in earlier fantasy and romance fiction, Mary Shelley's *Frankenstein* (1818) is the first major fictional exploration of the tragedy of misused technology, and specifically its disastrous consequences—as manifest in the construction of a monster—for the constitution of the human body. It is highly significant that so much of the horror in that book is a direct consequence of the bodily deformity of a man-made creature. This is underlined by the fact that the creature's one sustained friendship is with a blind man. The creature's deformity places him outside human society and its regulatory 'norms'. This not only drives him to acts of great violence, but also provides him with a unique position from which to view the operation of that society. As an acute observer of human society, he comes to recognise it as inherently unjust (Shelley, 1982:24). This first man-made creature is a fictional device for the description and critique of social injustice, including implicitly those misapplications of technology that have resulted in his own malformation.

Throughout the nineteenth century, social critics and observers continued to comment on the consequences for workers of using technology. Chartist poets such as Edward Mead, for example, wrote about the machine as a modern incarnation of the Ammonite god, Moloch, to whom children were thrown as living sacrifices.

> There is a King, and a ruthless King,
> Not a King of the poet's dream;
> But a tyrant fell, white slaves know well,
> And that ruthless King is Steam.

> He hath an arm, an iron arm,
> And tho' he hath but one,
> In that mighty arm there is a charm,
> That millions hath undone.
>
> Like the ancient Moloch grim, his sire
> In Himmon's vale that stood,
> His bowels are of living fire,
> And children are his food. (Mead, 1950:91)

Repeatedly the Chartists described the debilitating effects on the human operator obliged to interface with machines. In a newspaper called *The Labourer*, Ernest Jones wrote:

> The factories gave forth lurid fires
> From pent-up hells within their breast;
> E'en Aetna's burning wrath expires,
> But *man's* volcanoes never rest.
>
> Women, children, men were toiling,
> Locked in dungeons close and black,
> Life's fast-failing thread uncoiling
> Round the wheel, the *modern wrack*. (Jones, 1950:141)

Later in the nineteenth century Thomas Hardy and Richard Jeffries, who both wrote about country life and experience, presented similar fictional expositions of the physical distress caused by the operation of steam-powered agricultural machinery. In *Tess of the D'Urbervilles*, for example, Hardy gives a vivid picture of the plight of the worker operating the steam threshing-machine:

> She was the only woman whose place was upon the machine so as to be shaken bodily by its spinning . . . The incessant quivering, in which every fibre of her frame participated, had thrown her into a stupefied reverie in which her arms worked on independently of her consciousness. She hardly knew where she was . . . (Hardy, 1978:414)

Socialist critics such as William Morris echoed these concerns, commenting directly on changed perceptions of the human body, whose interface with industrial machinery had produced a new hybrid, the human-machine: 'If a man would live now, as a part of industrial economy, he must submit to be the hundredth part of a machine and swallow any longings he may have to exercise any special faculty' (Morris, 1885:49). As Morris notes, the problem is not simply with the debilitating physical effects of using large, inefficient, polluting and dangerous machines. He is equally concerned with the way in which the human body has been reconceptualised in this new technological age as part of a machine. For Morris this signifies a devaluation of what it meant to be human, brought about by the discursive and material exploitation of one class by another, and by the fetishisation of material wealth. In other words, Morris identifies a direct causal relation between political and social practice, between the uses of technology and the status and disposition of the human body.

Morris's concerns are reiterated in twentieth-century explorations of the relationship between human embodiment and technology, perhaps most powerfully by that successor to Victor Frankenstein's creature, the android or cyborg, but also in the production of other malformed or hybrid creatures as the result of chemical or biological experimentation. H. G. Wells's *The Island of Doctor Moreau* (1896) is an early fictional exploration of the effects of biological experimentation. Clumsily grafting human with animal components, Moreau produces hybrid beings incapable of maintaining and/or realising their humanity. Their struggles implicitly explore the relationship between humans and animals, particularly as mediated by modern technologies. While Wells's primary motivation here was undoubtedly his fascination with Darwinian science (as taught to him by T. H. Huxley), his problematic is particularly modern, given the development of techniques of genetic manipulation. Now that it is possible to modify the genetic materials of unborn babies, it is crucial to (re)conceptualise what is acceptably 'human'. In fact, it may be argued that this necessity has been present ever since refinements in pregnancy testing made it possible to detect specifiably 'abnormal' or 'unacceptable' kinds of human embodiment.

The other popular figure of technological manipulation is the android or cyborg. Part human and part machine (and therefore both mechanical and organic), these hybrid creatures—designed by humans—are characteristically driven by a need to define their humanity. Science fiction features various versions of this type. They include wholly mechanical robots which often do not look particularly human (such as Robby the Robot in *Forbidden Planet* (Fred M. Wilcox, 1956)); the android that is human in shape but still predominantly mechanical (Data in *Star Trek: the Next Generation*); the flesh–machine hybrid (the Schwarzenegger android of the *Terminator* movies); the genetically manipulated organic being (Nexus-6 of *Blade Runner*); and most recently the sophisticated polymer being of *Terminator 2*. Like Frankenstein's creation, the android is fetishised as the source of both superhuman power and subhuman limitations. Shelley's creature was extraordinarily strong and nimble, but also inhumanly ugly (the result of his having been composed of various ill-matched pieces of dead bodies). Because more recent androids have overcome some of the physical limitations of early nineteenth-century models and so look human, their exploration of humanity becomes all the more poignant. In *Blade Runner*, for example, a group of Nexus-6 androids are pursued by the blade runner, Rick Deckard, whose job is to destroy them before they commit any more acts of terrorism. The androids commit these terrorist acts in order to discover how to incapacitate their in-built self-destruct mechanisms; in their terms, they are fighting for their lives. Deckard, on the other hand, is working for authorities he does not respect, and for whom the androids' major 'crime' is to be bodily different from humans (Deckard's boss calls them 'skin jobs'). The movie's central problematic becomes therefore an exploration of the meaning of 'humanity': who is less human—the genetically-engineered androids who kill in order to live, or their human assassin who kills because he is ordered to? In fact, there are suggestions that the blade runner is himself an android (for like them he is preoccupied with family photographs which establish his 'human' past). Such similarities compound the moral dilemma posed in the movie.

The questions raised by the behaviour of the android characters and the moral dilemma of the blade runner concern the delineation of boundaries between the human and the machine. How much of the non-human is acceptable in the constitution of a 'human' body? Again, this line of questioning is not surprising at a time when technologies are rapidly changing, and consequently transforming our perception of the status and role of the human body. Human bodies in western societies have experienced already a great deal of technological intervention in the late twentieth century, notably as a result of medical and dental practice. If human bodies are so accommodating of prosthetic devices of various kinds, will there be a point at which what results is more prosthetic than human? And if so, what then will be its status? Although this is still largely in the realm of science fiction, it points nevertheless to questions with which all western societies are grappling. As microchip technologies become increasingly sophisticated and pervasive, it is important to consider how perceptions of 'the human' are affected. For example, as telephone technology becomes more complex and offers more on-line services, such as video access, it might be asked how this will influence common perceptions of such things as the relationship between public and private. And how will this in turn affect the status and function of the embodied subject operating the terminal? Already the extent to which mobile phone technology has altered perceptions of the mobility of human users and, subsequently, of bodily limitations might be analysed. It could be argued that the mobile phone has expanded the bodily potential of individual users by enabling them to move efficiently through space and time—rather like Arnold Schwarzenegger's Terminator—in the pursuit of particular goals (work or pleasure) formerly 'far beyond the realms of mortal men'.

Mark Poster offers a similar analysis of the cyborg cop in the Paul Verhoeven film, *RoboCop*:

> It has become a truism that the body is always already culturally inscribed, never a natural object available without mediation for a rational subject (of science). The complication I want to introduce is this: industrial society and now 'postindustrial' society, the mode of production and now the mode of information, have inserted into the social space analogues of the human body in the form of increasingly complex tools. (Poster, 1992:437)

Murphy, the police officer become cyborg, is for Poster one such tool, an embodiment of this 'new species of cyborgs and androids' which now exist in a specular, mirroring relation to human beings (ibid.). As in the *Terminator* movies, the background to *RoboCop* is the Hollywood movie industry, with its production for profit of violent escapist movies. But it is also more than this: 'something new is added that, at one level, reinforces these themes, and, at another level, undermines them: new discursive practices of the mode of information now take the lead in controlling and empowering the body' (ibid.:439). In the movie, as in life, the battle is for control of the information fed into the body, or rather into selected bodies: 'The outcome of the drama rests with the question of who will best manipulate the capabilities of the mode of information—the bad guys (Dick Jones et al.) or the good guys (Murphy and his partner, Lewis)?' (ibid.:439). It is significant here that the good guys include Murphy, the RoboCop's human component, who might otherwise lose control of his corporeality and yield its power to the bad guys.

It has been noted of late that the information superhighway is not so much a freeway as a toll-way, and that the only people certain to access it will be the toll-paying few. This is not to say, however, that everyone else will be untouched by this new technology; it means rather that they will be reconstituted, disembodied, and re-embodied in order to fit the demands of a new technological mode. At its most frightening, this entails loss of control over embodiment, as when Murphy is in danger of losing himself to the bad guys in *RoboCop*. The television android Data (of *Star Trek: the Next Generation*) sometimes enacts the same concern. Data is a 'good guy'. As second officer of the starship *Enterprise*, his superhuman powers and abilities—rapid information-processing, great strength, very swift reflexes—are utilised for the common good. On one particular journey, however, the *Enterprise* crew discovers that Data has a twin, Lore, whose primary motivation is access to power. The problem for the *Enterprise* crew is that Data and Lore, being made from the same mould (literally), are physically indistinguishable. The havoc wrought by Lore when he deactivates and then impersonates Data warns us of the danger of a technology out of (human) control. In fact, Lore's manipulation of Data—and the terrifying loss of identity it signifies—is the most disturbing feature of the episode.

These fears of manipulation and loss of bodily integrity are enacted most spectacularly in the 'bad' Terminator of *Terminator 2*. Labelled T1000, he is a Liquid Metal Terminator, made from a 'mimetic polyalloy' which has the properties of mercury, and is able to adopt any shape with the same volume as his own. The original Terminator (played by Arnold Schwarzenegger) was a Cyberdine Systems Model T101 made of flesh over a metal endoskeleton, which maintained a skeletal human shape even when all the skin was stripped away. But by contrast the Liquid Metal Terminator constantly violates the boundaries of the 'normal' human body: he can extrude parts of himself into blades with which to pierce human bodies; he can camouflage himself as either a human body or a tiled floor, and he is able to reconstitute himself when blasted apart or broken into very small pieces. He makes the Schwarzenegger model seem almost friendly by comparison; in fact, in *Terminator 2* the Arnie cyborg actually defends John and Sarah Conner from their Liquid Metal pursuer.

This second Terminator dramatises a series of concerns about the loss of bodily integrity, and the stability and reliability of certain kinds of embodied identities. T1000 spends almost the entire movie in the dress of an American motorcycle police officer, complete with helmet, mirrored sunglasses, and crisp shirt tucked into elasticised pants. He is played by an actor with extremely well-defined, clean-cut and handsome features. It is noteworthy that his characterisation is primarily an embodiment; he speaks very little throughout the movie, and then often in the voices of those whose bodies he has counterfeited. In one reading he is a version of one of the Village People, a gay identity signified by his dress and impeccable grooming. In this persona the cyborg might be seen as acting out fears about AIDS and HIV, that virus which enters the body and destroys it from within, and which is commonly associated with gay culture. His body-piercing attacks—aimed mostly at men, and projected through body cavities such as the mouth and eyes—might then be read as dramatisations of homophobic attitudes often associated with AIDS/HIV hysteria.

In both his polymorphousness and his ability to occupy the bodies of others, T1000 may also be seen as dramatising concerns about a technology that can enter the body (with or without consent) and act on it at the cellular level from within. In a sense, this is what viruses do. But nanotechnologists now predict the development of machines so small that they can be injected into the body via the bloodstream. Although their uses have yet to be determined, optimally they might be used to combat disease—as did the miniaturised submariners of *Fantastic Voyage* (Richard Fleischer, 1966). Such applications are extreme predictions of the new technologies with which western society is already dealing, and which are already changing western perceptions of the body. Consider, for example, the use of intra-uterine probes such as ultrasound, amniocentesis, and chorionic villus sampling for the medical assessment of foetuses. On the one hand, they can be seen as offering women exactly the information they need in order to make informed decisions about their own bodies (such as whether a pregnancy should be terminated). On the other hand, it must be recognised that such procedures are a new form of bodily regulation and control, a new means of policing the definition of an 'acceptable' human embodiment. Furthermore, their use relieves a society from having to deal with those who are differently embodied, or even to examine its collective unwillingness or inability to provide a worthwhile life for such citizens. These procedures are also implicated, of course, in the selection of children by sex, and the abortion of foetuses because they are female—a practice which many would see as a blatant abuse of the technology. The point is that each use of these technologies (whether for good or ill, depending on the perspectives taken) involves an intrusion which then becomes a means of regulating and controlling both the maternal body (to abort or not) and the body of the foetus (to be aborted or sustained). Given traditional assumptions about bodily integrity in western society (where the most violent action is the violation of someone else's body), it seems inevitable that such practices—even when performed with the best motives—will provoke unease.

With respect to both the dis-ease of AIDS and the un-ease of high-tech medicine, the Liquid Terminator can be seen as an embodiment of anxieties about the penetration and violation of the human body, as well as about the consequences of such violation for the ongoing (re)conceptualisation of the body over which we as individual embodied subjects have little control. T1000 enacts comparable concerns at the loss of certainty about embodied identities. One of the most disturbing features of his characterisation is surely his police officer persona. To look at, he is an ideal representative of the law and of the State: clean-cut, handsome and well-dressed in a recognisable and respected uniform, he seems a stereotypical embodiment of the State's protective and regulatory function. Yet he acts like a thug. He is a murderer who seems to enjoy the perversity of his actions, particularly in the scenes of body penetration. By contrast, the conventional image of the corrupt police officer is a character such as Lieutenant Eckhardt in *Batman* (Tim Burton, 1989). Overweight, unkempt and unshaven, he is constituted by signifiers which place him outside late twentieth-century bodily definitions of 'normal' or 'good'. But because T1000 looks like he should be a good guy, his character is even more disturbing. He resembles 'one of us' (the good people), whereas, like Eckhardt, he should look like 'one of them' (a criminal).

The late twentieth century is a time not only of rapid technological change in the west, but also of rapid political and social change. The introduction of anti-discrimination and equal opportunity laws, the huge migrations resulting from wars, the breakdown of nineteenth-century colonial regimes, the demands on sovereign territories of multinational capitalism, the increased reach of literacy and numeracy, and the infiltration of middle-class institutions by members of traditionally working-class families are just some of the social and political developments that have radically altered western society. Accordingly, many nineteenth-century values which once constituted the moral and ethical basis of bourgeois society in the west have since proved unsustainable, based as they are on racial, ethnic, class, gender, age and sexual inequalities which are generally unacceptable nowadays. It is no longer possible to characterise an individual socially at a glance, though there are always many markers for doing so. As with the Liquid Terminator, the problem is that too often mistakes are made. Individual and institutional identities are suddenly permeable and flexible, where once they seemed solid and impregnable. The hybrid human–machine can be seen as embodying this uncertainty and anxiety, but also perhaps the possibilities it opens up.

## Cyborg manifesto: (re)positioning the cyborg

In her celebrated essay, 'A Cyborg Manifesto' (1991), Donna Haraway argues that a cyborg imaginary can usefully challenge what Jacques Derrida calls the 'phallogocentrism' of late twentieth-century western capitalist society. In her view the old dualisms that structure western thought have finally broken down by being 'techno-digested', a term she adopts from Zoe Sofia (Sofoulis) (Haraway, 1991:163). What results is the loss of old identities and the formation of new hybrid positionings, which people occupy strategically in order to position themselves powerfully enough to protect their own interests. Accordingly, Haraway proposes replacing the imagery of private and public 'domains'—the 'places' of women and men—with the image of networking: 'I prefer a network ideological image, suggesting the profusion of spaces and identities and the permeability of boundaries in the personal body and the body politic. "Networking" is both a feminist practice and a multinational corporate strategy—weaving is for oppositional cyborgs' (ibid.:170). Furthermore, she argues that the most effective strategy for women is to learn how to read and then deconstruct these networks, in the process constructing new kinds of identities not bound by earlier dichotomies:

> there is no 'place' for women in these networks, only geometrics of difference and contradiction crucial to women's cyborg identities. If we learn how to read these webs of power and social life, we might learn new couplings, new coalitions. There is no way to read the following list [of what she calls key social sites] from a standpoint of 'identification', of a unitary self. The issue is dispersion. The task is to survive the diaspora. (ibid.)

For Haraway the cyborg serves as a metaphorical expression of the dissolution of boundaries—social, economic, political, and corporeal. In so doing, it challenges traditionally corporeal or embodied definitions of humanity, which cannot engage successfully with the new 'informatics of domination'. This is Haraway's term for the regime of those new information-based technologies which effectively are determining the economic, social, political and corporeal form(ul)ations of humanity.

> Our bodies, ourselves; bodies are maps of power and identity. Cyborgs are no exception. A cyborg body is not innocent; it was not born in a garden; it does not seek unitary identity and so generate antagonistic dualisms without end (or until the world ends); it takes irony for granted. One is too few, and two is only one possibility. Intense pleasure in skill, machine skill, ceases to be a sin, but an aspect of our embodiment. We can be responsible for machines; *they* do not dominate or threaten us. We are responsible for boundaries; we are they. (ibid.:180)

Haraway's somewhat utopian vision makes the point that even technologies such as these offer spaces of opposition, which can be utilised in a new kind of politics based not on the rejection of socio-economic and technological change, but on its acceptance and subsequent remodelling. To speak of the information 'network' as a 'web' is one such transposition; it renders the network susceptible to a feminist revisioning, because the web or tapestry has long been associated metaphorically with feminine power. More fundamentally, Haraway argues that we should accept the implicitly cyborg embodiment of the new informatics as a source of more complex, shifting, and fluid identities. Her reason is that these can be aligned strategically in the interests of both the individual and groups of individuals, so as to overcome the limitations of old-style essentialist alliances which are marked inevitably by repressions and silences (ibid.:156). This (re)positioning of the cyborg, Haraway acknowledges, is a reworking of Chela Sandoval's notion of an 'oppositional consciousness', which 'marks out a self-consciously constructed space that cannot affirm the capacity to act on the basis of natural identification, but only on the basis of conscious coalition, of affinity, of political kinship' (ibid.:155). Like the cyborg, 'we are responsible for boundaries' and thus 'we are they' (ibid.:180).

## Wet-ware: infotech and embodiment

Having discussed the most positive revisions of the cyborg as infotech 'embodiment', it is necessary now to raise certain concerns about this new phase of socio-economic, political and everyday life. Haraway's essay includes an analysis of some of the fictional writing which most readily expresses the cyborg identities she discusses. This includes work by writers such as Anne McCaffrey, Vonda McIntyre, Samuel Delany, and Joanna Russ. The writer whose fiction most obviously challenges the chimeric identities of that post-techno and postmodern world envisioned by Haraway is William Gibson.

Gibson's novel, *Neuromancer* (1986), is not concerned with the merging and blending of identities and positionings (by sex, gender, race, ethnicity, class, age) into a new kind of embodiment. Instead it celebrates the 'liberation' of the mind from the 'confines' of the body: 'For Case, who'd lived for the bodiless exultation of cyberspace, it was the Fall. In the bars he'd frequented as a cowboy hotshot, the elite stance involved a certain relaxed contempt for the flesh. The body was meat. Case fell into the prison of his own flesh' (Gibson, 1986:12). As either 'meat' or 'wet-ware' (as distinct from the hardware and software of information technology), the body is perceived in Platonic terms as a 'prison'. Cyberspace—that virtual space in which PC-users meet and exchange information or just snoop around—is then a utopian environment which one can explore unimpeded by embodiment. This is a conceptualisation of infotech-use that reinforces rather than deconstructs the mind/body dichotomy. Certainly, the inhabitants of Gibson's high-tech world play with their own embodiment. In *Neuromancer* much is made of the implants and body grafts of the post-punk high-jackers or 'console cowboys' with whom Case, the main character, deals. Yet this cosmetic manipulation of the body serves mainly to fetishise the realm of the non-corporeal: the body is 'meat' to be manipulated by will, which is the realm of the mind. Case becomes so preoccupied with his time in cyberspace that he forgets to eat. The body is 'meat' because it is a nuisance. The enjoyments it offers—sex, and shared-body experiences via broadcast implants—are minor compared to the joy and challenge of travel in the abstract realm of cyberspace.

In 'A Cyborg Manifesto' Haraway writes briefly about video game culture as a model for the construction of a new 'private space': 'The culture of video games is heavily orientated to individual competition and extraterrestrial warfare. High-tech, gendered imaginations are produced here, imaginations that can contemplate destruction of the planet and a sci-fi escape from its consequences . . . These are the technologies that promise ultimate mobility and perfect exchange . . .' (ibid.:168). *Neuromancer* refers at some length to this 'private space', although it is much more than a fictional rendition of that space and the masculinist imagination which inhabits it in disembodied form. This is not so much a new space as a very old one to which the PC-user (or Virtual Reality occupant) has new access. It is a space not for the refiguring of embodiment, but for its denigration as 'meat' and 'wet-ware'. The problem for the console cowboy is to remember to keep alive the body which allows him access to a disembodied space totally dependent, paradoxically, on the body. Marge Piercy's cyberspace travellers in *Body of Glass* (1991) experience the same difficulty. The image of rows of VR travellers stretched out on beds as they experience virtual reality is perhaps an updated version of opium-den scenes, and just as disconcerting. In the ZOO-TV video-movie, Bono—the lead singer of the Irish rock group, U2—noted that he first became aware of the need to intervene in the use of this new technology when he heard a soldier talking about his job as a weapons-console operator during the Gulf War. At the end of his shift, the soldier was asked on camera what it had been like to launch and guide a series of successful attacks on Iraqi targets. He responded that it had been very exciting because it seemed 'real'. For this soldier, the bodily consequences of the advanced video game in which he was involved ('extraterrestrial warfare', as Haraway calls it) were not an issue, because the mind-set he was operating with was not 'reality' but a game. For him, the mind/body dualism was still clearly in operation.

Case's travels in cyberspace in *Neuromancer* have similar components of delight and astonishment. In other ways, Case experiences the nagging stress of the corporeal; not just because he is (possibly) being slowly poisoned as the result of chemical implants. Yet this novel is characterised predominantly by its vision of the pleasures afforded by disembodiment, and not least for a wholly individuated and individualistic life devoid of corporeal constraints and responsibilities. In a sense this takes us straight back to *Frankenstein*'s narrative of the devastating consequences of rejecting corporeal responsibility for technology. There the rejected—the monstrous-other—are the working classes of nineteenth-century Britain, and (in another metaphorical reading) women. In *Neuromancer*, the alienated are the deskilled workers who have lost their jobs as the result of this new technology, and they include both middle-class and working-class men and women. In fact, as Haraway notes, the current pattern of deskilling and unemployment is quite different from what it was in the previous industrial revolution (Haraway, 1991:166). At the beginning of *Neuromancer*, Case has lost his ability to operate in cyberspace; he is one of the deskilled. The novel is less concerned with the story of that deskilling, however, than with his joy at being restored to the work-force, which enables him to experience the particular pleasures of a kind of 'work' that involves disembodied travels through the Net. Nevertheless, subversive possibilities are raised, such as 'shared' embodiments produced by the broadcasting of an individual's sensory responses.

*Neuromancer* was, and to some extent still is, at the cutting edge in exploring these new technologies. It fictionalises a range of different concerns and debates, although (as responses to it attest) it mainly celebrates the achievement of the Platonic and Augustinian objective of freedom from the prison of the flesh. The triumph of mind over body, and the constitution of the body as an abhorrent material prison, are traditionally masculine preoccupations, which may account for the predominance of male-users of high technology. In particular, it might be argued, cyberspace offers teenage boys relief from the terrors of their embodiment during the stresses of male puberty. Recently women have begun to enter this male preserve, some (such as the Adelaide-based art group, VNS Matrix) with the stated objective of disrupting the male dominance (and consequent phallocentrism) of the information technology field.

## Rhizome versus gap: new conceptualisations of desire

It is useful to consider which metaphor of desire is most applicable to those revised notions of humanity and community brought about by this new technology. For when individuals are dispersed and reconstituted as part of a network of behaviours and activities, desire is likely to be figured as cybernetic. This makes it different from that currently popular Freudian–Lacanian concept of desire, which explains it by reference to the linguistic figure of metonymy: 'It is the movement from one signifier to another, which Lacan claims is the very movement of *desire,* the endless substitution of one object of desire for another, none of which is adequate to fill the original lack propelling desire—the lost or renounced mother' (Grosz, 1989:24). This notion of desire as a lack to be filled is made obsolete in the network, where the opening of a gap results instantly in a re-routing (of information, of sensory and perceptual feedback, and so on) through other available channels.

To abandon the Freudian–Lacanian conception of desire is to relieve individuals placed within such a structure of dichotomous experiences. No longer is there lover and beloved, active and passive, subject and object, male and female. Instead, we have the possibility of different gratifications, the reconstitution of desire in different forms and not necessarily policed in the same old ways. Cyberpunk writers have explored these conceptualisations. In *Psion* (1982) and *Catspaw* (1988) Joan D. Vinge uses her principal character, Cat, to explore the cyborg interfaces discussed by Haraway. Cat is a natural 'psion'; that is, he has the ability to enter the cyberspace of individual consciousnesses. Furthermore, he discovers that he can also enter the cyberspace of information technologies. In a sense, Cat is the apotheosis of the cyborg: he is no longer an analog, but a digital being; because he is also flesh, he is a perfect fusion of human and machine ability. The source of this 'natural' ability is his alien heritage, embodied in his cat-shaped eyes. The alien race from which he is descended was destroyed in genocidal attacks by Earth people frightened of their psionic ability. Cat discovers that the terror which prevents him from accessing his powers is the memory of his mother being beaten to death because of her alienness. Through his ability to interface with both human and technological cyberspace, Cat is able to explore and deconstruct those regulatory dichotomies that have determined his life: human versus alien, human versus machine. In other words, Vinge uses her principal character to explore a series of dualisms regularly used in the social construction of alienness or otherness. Cat is positioned in a network of different identities that serially constitute his various positionings within the society in which he moves. Each has its own possibilities, its own potential for desire.

In that case, to figure desire as a 'network' or 'rhizome' seems to be an unequivocally positive move, and utopian in western terms in the potentials it offers for greater democracy, and for less rigid and less easily regulated identities and social positionings. This is why it is important to ensure that this vision does not collapse into a readily manipulated, politically and socially unselfconscious pluralism. Haraway notes that Chela Sandoval's 'oppositional consciousness is about contradictory locations and heterochronic calendars, not about relativisms and pluralisms' (Haraway, 1991:155–6). The danger is that this reconceptualised notion of desire, individual positioning and community may result in the simplistic notion that the openness of the network leads inevitably to democracy. It is interesting to note how often this notion of inevitable democratisation appears in the advertising of major computer companies and associated industries. In 1993, the popular infotech magazine *Wired* featured the following quotation from an article by one its contributors, illustrated and spread across three of its opening pages: 'Life in cyberspace is more egalitarian than elitist, more decentralized than hierarchical . . . It serves individuals and communities, not mass audiences . . . We might think of life in cyberspace as shaping up exactly like Thomas Jefferson would have wanted it: founded on the primacy of individual liberty and a commitment to pluralism, diversity, and community' (*Wired,* 1993:23–5). It is a possibility, but no more than that. The development of publishing technologies and the spread of literacy also promised greater democracy, and in some senses that promise can be seen to have been fulfilled (particularly if one does not examine the meaning of 'democracy' too closely). Yet the same skills and technologies also enabled the development of more effective means of social regulation and control, inscribed not just in the pages of law books but on the bodies of individual citizens (as Franz Kafka illustrates so effectively in his story, 'In the Penal Colony' (1948)). Contemporary technological developments like the Internet, nanotechnologies and genetic testing and manipulation all offer the potential for exploring new and different identities, new ways of operating within society, and new conceptualisations of individual embodiment. But they are also concerned with the codification and more rigid regulation and control of traditional western values, including the dichotomous constitution of the body as the negative other of mind, as is most apparent in much cyberpunk literature and in VR fantasies. Twentieth-century technologies have already transformed western understanding of the nature of human embodiment in, for example, space–time. Equally important is the potential of this technology to eradicate the traditional western dichotomies of sex, gender, class, race, ethnicity, age, and so on. The challenge is neither a relativism nor pluralism which all too easily becomes the realm of those who control the technology. Rather it is to identify the 'contradictory locations' of Sandoval's model, and use them to weaken the control of those traditional dichotomies, which, by perpetuating the negative power of 'otherness', impede an understanding of 'difference':

> Now the humans had built their own Net, and it was techno-genetic, cruder but stronger. And now they were using it to climb inexorably up the same ever-steepening evolutionary curve . . . I thought about Elnear again: about the chosen few already on the brink of something unknowable . . . and all the systems within systems below them, the individual humans who had become the core—the soul, Elnear had said—of an evolving meta-being they called a combine, creating their future almost without realising it.
>
> Maybe they'd never take the final step, either; maybe for humans it would always be too hard. Maybe the fear of Otherness that was always there, inside a mind that could never really put itself in somebody else's place, would always hold them back. Or maybe they'd make it just because they'd had to fight so hard simply to survive; because they'd never given up trying to bridge the impossible gulf between one human mind and another . . . (Vinge, 1988:453)

6

# Conclusion: The Body in the Text

The sarcophagus is one of the earliest examples of the body as a text. Entombed in a coffin inscribed biographically, often embalmed (and with its organs stored adjacently in stone pots), the body of an ancient noble is narrativised for the edification of posterity. This early example of the disruption and dispersal of bodily integrity is separated by only a few thousand years from contemporary accounts of the fragmentation of identity, and the radical reconceptualisation of the body in an era characterised by the development of new technologies such as infotech, robotics and genetic engineering. The period in between is marked by a series of inventions and reinventions of the nature of corporeality. The intensified interest in 'the body' at this time in western societies is an expression of several different concerns. First, the possibilities of new social and political positionings (produced by changes in western society) necessitate a reformulation of the nature of individual identity, which traditionally has been recognised as bodily inscribed. Secondly, the information technologies which have transformed life in the west in the last half century or more are themselves bodily inscribed, and are altering western formulations of the nature of human embodiment.

This final chapter canvasses several areas in which theoretical preoccupations with the body are opening up new areas of analysis, and either offering different perspectives on old questions or asking questions that formerly could not have been asked at all.

Some of these have been mentioned in preceding chapters, but this is a final opportunity to touch on certain issues, debates and concerns which a necessarily abbreviated account cannot deal with in full. The next section considers some recent writings on the performance arts of music and dance, because they bring different (but complementary) perspectives to the debates already described. Following this is a section on embodiments of new masculinities and femininities which, interestingly enough, are equally as apparent in texts dealing with the new technologies as in texts which directly consider new (en)genderings of subjectivity.

## The body and/as the text

The role of the body in the perception and reception of music is an area of increasing interest and debate. Although the notion of a relationship between bodily and musical characteristics is not new, it has tended to be formulated traditionally in terms of the dichotomies discussed in the opening chapter. Contemporary (re)readings of that relationship and of what constitutes music are very different. Sally Macarthur concludes an article which explores the impact of feminism on musicology with this formulation:

> Music's body is my body in a state of music. Music is in my (h)ear(ing), in my (h)ear(t), in my ear. Music is a throbbing, pulsating body, a feminised woman's body . . . the musical body, the feminised Other, wraps (it)self around my body, my feminised female body, ambiguous and unable to be defined (another version of Irigaray's 'this sex which is not one') . . . made up of one and many identities simultaneously, the musical body becomes mine and mine its (hers). (Macarthur, 1994:16)

This reformulation of the body as active participant in music is an important move in the analysis of conservative music ideologies, which make no space for feminine participation in the reception and production of music. Equally, the notion that the body of the performer is actively involved in its production involves revaluing many assumptions about the nature of 'good' music. If, for example, the body of the performer inscribes the music she is simultaneously inscribed by while producing, then differences in embodiment will result in a proscriptive view of what constitutes quality in music, and these will inevitably disadvantage those occupying marginalised social positionings. Furthermore, it is arguable that the lower status accorded some musical genres (blues, rock'n'roll) rather than others (classical, orchestral, and opera) reflects the social status of both performers and audiences as mediated via the music (Shepherd, 1991:164–71; Cranny-Francis, 1994:46–8). To write the body into the music text is therefore an important strategy in the development of what Macarthur and others call 'the new musicology'.

Dance is another field in which the body obviously plays a major part. Yet there is a sense in which traditional notions of dance have fetishised movement at great cost to the embodied performer, in so far as stylised movements have been considered more important, powerful and beautiful than the bodies of those who performed them. Developments in dance in the twentieth century have not eschewed movement technique, but in their most radical forms they have given priority to the human body which produces those movements. Elizabeth Dempster gives the following account:

> Literacy in dance, from which a critical reading proceeds, must begin with attention to the body and to the gravity, levity, spatiality and rhythms of its movement. When the object speaks, when the body dances, perhaps it is not a watching but a listening which is required. Or if it is a watching, it is watching with an eye that glides under the surface of skin and rests there, listening without expectation. We need to learn to look critically at the body in dance and to resist the seductions of the glittering surface, of old stories and old bodies in new clothes. I have likened this vigilant watching to a process of dissection: it is an incisive glance that destroys the deceptive unity of the dancing body. But in this act of incision another, evanescent body is born. (Dempster, 1988:52)

Dempster goes on to describe the subversive potential of this revisioning of dance when it comes into conflict with academic dance practice, which is conservative and gendered masculine:

> The realm of the 'proper' is his body, his dance, his speech. To speak his tongue she leaves her mother and hands her body

> over to the academy. For the rest of us, we have no option but to be 'improper', to speak pidgin, to mutter, to stammer, and to block up our ears against his bitter scorn. But sometimes in an unguarded moment a fissure opens in a once silent body and from it flows an unstoppable, uncontainable speaking as we cast our bodies without thinking into space. (ibid.)

Dempster's elegant evocation of subversive performance might apply equally well to a number of other practices, artistic and otherwise, as well as to other subversive positionings (for example, post-colonialist, or anti-bourgeois) in relation to those practices. The notion, developed by the French feminist Hélène Cixous, of *l'écriture feminine* (feminine writing), for example, might be restated in these terms, as a refusal of the languages and genres of the academic mainstream. Replacing them is a writing practice which is partly metatextual (that is, fundamentally critical of mainstream writing) but equally the expression of a body which refuses to be positioned, regulated and controlled by the mainstream. In this respect, the body itself is as metatextual as the writing.

## Embodying new femininities and masculinities

We move now from metatextual to metasexual bodies as represented in contemporary explorations of new kinds of femininity and masculinity which challenge the traditional and conservative stereotypes. One of the most striking features of *Terminator 2*, which uses cyborgs to explore the effects of technologisation on bodies, is the embodiment of Sarah Conner, the female hero of the original Terminator movie. In *The Terminator* Sarah was a very sweet, slim, and attractive woman with curly brown hair. As the mother of the future earth-saviour, John Conner, she was a Madonna figure (in the Biblical sense) to be protected at all costs. Yet it was she who, as a mother protecting her child, delivered the final blow to the CS101 cyborg. In *Terminator 2* Conner is totally involved in the mother-protector role, but the Sarah Conner encountered by the audience is this time a very different figure. Dressed in combat gear, she spends her time in the asylum in which she has been incarcerated training herself physically to defend her son. She is now almost anorexically thin, and impressively muscled—a kind of feminine counterpart to the overdeveloped Schwarzenegger. In fact, one of the principal sources of media attention when *Terminator 2* was first released was the reinscription of Conner. The debate concerned whether or not her femininity had been compromised by her prominent musculature and unfeminine emotions (she rarely exhibits stereotypically 'feminine' feelings, but more often powerfully 'masculine' passions, such as revenge and ruthless determination).

The characterisation of Sarah Conner enacts a number of ongoing debates about the 'nature' of femininity and masculinity. *Terminator 2* was made and released at a time when rock stars such as Madonna were challenging the traditional passivity and physical softness of feminine stereotypes. Yet there was also at this time a backlash against feminism for challenging those same stereotypes: one version of it was a series of movies in which the women who adopted powerful roles were either insane or absolutely ruthless, for example *Fatal Attraction* (Adrian Lyne, 1987) and *Basic Instinct* (Paul Verhoeven, 1992). The characterisation of Conner does not seem part of this backlash, because the reason that she develops such dominant characteristics as physical strength, knowledge of weapons, emotional toughness and mechanical ingenuity (all formerly the province of men) is the conventionally feminine motive of maternal protectiveness. In other words, her characterisation offers viewers an interesting problem in the form of a different femininity, defined in terms which are both traditionally masculine and traditionally feminine, and so unable to be subsumed into either category.

*Terminator 2*'s construction of the new nuclear family (Sarah Conner, John Conner, and CS101, the Schwarzenegger cyborg) is part of this same exploration of new engenderings and new sexual identities. Ironically, this 'nuclear' family prevents the nuclear holocaust which would have destroyed Earth's future: this makes them an (anti-)nuclear family, perhaps. At one point in the movie Sarah is shown musing on the relationship between John and CS101, noting (via voice-over) that she need not worry about providing John with a father, since the cyborg (whom she calls 'the machine') will be totally caring and loyal in a way that a human father might not be. As to whether this (re)constituted family can experience an intimate relationship between mother and father, the movie offers no hint. So this is a family without sex. CS101 is a new man—impressive in stereotypical masculine terms (big, with well-defined muscles, a conventionally short hair-cut, strong, square features, a big gun, and a motorcycle)—but sexless. Even in *The Terminator* there was no threat of sexual violence against Sarah Conner, but instead 'just' a death-threat which may be read as confirming a heterosexist regime sustained by implicit (and actual) threats of violence against women by men. The *Terminator 2* family may then be read as a deconstructive vision not only of late twentieth-century relations between men and women but also of the nuclear family itself—as well as expressing a number of anxieties about the development of new masculinities and femininities. For example, if CS101 is a version of the 'new man'—caring for and protective of children, and a battle companion of the boy's mother—then it is disturbing that he is sexless. Furthermore, if the 'new woman' who is physically assertive and emotionally tough can live companionably only with an automaton, then this does not offer such women much hope for the future.

If the super-bodies of the last two decades or so (muscle-builders such as Schwarzenegger, and super-models such as Elle Macpherson) repeatedly attest to a preoccupation with redefining masculinity and femininity, so too do the stories of physical breakdown, particularly the narratives of anorexia which regularly appear in magazines and on television (in current affairs, news and talk-show programmes). The anorexia stories are interestingly double-focused. On the one hand, stories about the stress experienced by women (and some men) in attempting to fashion themselves in terms of a social ideal are useful deconstructions of that ideal. On the other hand, it is equally important to consider the role of such stories in promoting a particular version of femininity. As Abigail Bray concludes in her article, 'The Edible Woman':

> Not only are women framed as suffering from an eating disorder but, perhaps more importantly, from a reading disorder in which to see an image of the 'self' is to end up like Narcissus. At work within the discourses on anorexia is a suspiciously undemocratic infantilisation of the female audience as pathologically susceptible

> to media images . . . Without tolling the bell of doom, it appears that what we are witnessing within popular discourses on eating disorders is the pathologisation of women's everyday lives. (Bray, 1994:9)

Movies such as *Terminator 2* suggest that men's lives are also being pathologised in a counter-move against the opening-up of debates about gendered identities and embodied sex. Their 'new man' options include the sexless CS101 or the violent, transgressive, gay-identified T1000. At the same time, traditional masculine roles are confirmed in the film as inadequate: the abusive psychiatric nurse, for instance, as well as John Conner's chauvinistic working-class foster-father, and the smug psychiatrist who authorised Sarah Conner's imprisonment and refuses her pleas to see her son. In fact, the sympathetic male characters in the film are all positioned in some way as 'different' or 'other': examples include the Latin American gun-dealer whom Sarah Conner meets in the desert, and the middle-class African-American scientist who developed the cyborg for Cyberdine Industries, and who dies destroying his own work. In other words, in order to challenge the authoritarian preoccupations of traditional masculine stereotypes, some positioning as 'other' seems to be required.

*Terminator 2* does not redefine the nature of contemporary masculinity and femininity; nor does it set out to. However, by fetishising the body as cybernetic, masculine and feminine, it constitutes a site for exploring some fundamental concerns of contemporary theorists of the body.

## The body in the text

I began this study by noting the disparate sources of contemporary interest in and theorisation of the body. On the one hand, politicised writers are working on the bodily inscription of social markers such as gender, sexuality, class, race, ethnicity and age; on the other hand, postmodernist writers are exploring the reconceptualisation of the body under the influence of information technologies. For all of these theorists, the body is not only part of or 'in' their own texts, but is also inscribed by the texts of the markers and practices—social and technological—they are exploring. No central concern draws all these theorists into some kind of 'grand narrative' of the body. Nevertheless, they all contribute in different ways, and for different reasons, to the dissolution of conservative notions of the body as a coherent and unified entity, defined and regulated by a range of hierarchised dualisms, such as male/female, white/black, mind/body, human/alien, human/machine, human/animal. Instead, we are presented with a polymorphous body, which explores the boundaries of gender, sexuality, class, race, ethnicity, age, and the interactions between humans and machines. Because of the fluid nature of the social reality in which it exists and functions, the polymorphous body is obliged to engage in this exploration. Individual bodies which are (or attempt to be) passive or inactive will be repositioned by the social, political, economic and technological life in which they are immersed. So there is a sense in which passivity is an impossibility. The body is in the text of everyday life; by enacting that text, it becomes not a product but the processor of everyday life.

The popular texts of everyday life, as well as the theorists who critique both everyday life and its texts, work to detect and to define those potentialities and possibilities made available by changing social and technological conditions. As the work of such theorists attests, the body is inscribed by the positionings it is assigned and enacts; it is assigned to positionings by the inscriptions it exhibits; it is positioned technologically in a community for whom these inscriptions may or may not have meanings. Virtually all these theorists, novelists and film-makers agree that the major challenge is not to remake the past in its own image. A common aim is to remake the body in new and different ways, in order to remedy those inequitable practices of the past which have been written so clearly on the bodies of the dispossessed, the victimised and the abused. The embodied subject has a different role in our changing society. Instead of maintaining old distinctions and their regulatory definitions, it tactically occupies a range of different positionings that enable it to subvert those remainders and reminders —both institutional and individual—of traditional, inequitable discourses and social practices. As the psion, Cat notes: 'Nothing's changed—yet. But it will. I got a few lives I ain't even tried yet' (Vinge, 1982:214).

# Bibliography

## Printed sources

Allen, Judith and Elizabeth Grosz (eds) (1987) *Australian Feminist Studies Special Issue: Feminism and the Body* 5

Allen, Judith and Paul Patton (eds) (1983) *Beyond Marxism? Interventions After Marx*, Sydney: Intervention

Althusser, Louis (1971) 'Ideology and Ideological State Apparatuses' in *Lenin and Philosophy and Other Essays*, trans. Ben Brewster, New York: Monthly Review Press

Arnold, David (1988) 'Touching the Body: Perspectives on the Indian Plague, 1896–1900' in Ranajit Guha and Gayatri Chakravorty Spivak (eds) *Selected Subaltern Studies*, New York and Oxford: Oxford University Press, pp. 391–426

Attfield, Judy and Pat Kirkham (eds) (1989) *A View from the Interior: Feminism, Women and Design*, London: Women's Press

Barr, Marlene S. (1992) *Feminist Fabulation: Space/Postmodern Fiction*, Iowa City: University of Iowa Press

—— (1993) *Lost in Space: Probing Feminist Science Fiction and Beyond*, Chapel Hill and London: University of North Carolina Press

Bernstein, Basil (1975) *Class, Codes and Control: Volume 3 Towards a Theory of Educational Transmissions*, 2nd edn, London: Routledge and Kegan Paul

Bhabha, Homi K. (1990) 'The Other Question: Difference, Discrimination and the Discourse of Colonialism', in Ferguson et al. (eds) *Out There*, pp. 71–87 [1984]

Bordo, Susan (1988) 'Anorexia Nervosa: Psychopathology as the Crystallization of Nature' in Irene Diamond and Lee Quimby (eds) *Feminism and Foucault: Reflections on Resistance*, Boston: Northeastern University Press, pp. 87–118

Bourdieu, Pierre (1984) *Distinction: A Social Critique of the Judgement of Taste*, trans. Richard Nice, London: Routledge and Kegan Paul [Fr 1979]

—— (1988) *Homo Academicus*, trans. Peter Collier, Cambridge: Polity [Fr 1984]

Bray, Abigail (1994) 'The Edible Woman: Reading/Eating Disorders and Femininity', *Media Information Australia* 72, pp. 3–10

Butler, Judith (1990) *Gender Trouble: Feminism and the Subversion of Identity*, New York and London: Routledge

—— (1993) *Bodies That Matter: On the Discursive Limits of 'Sex'*, New York: Routledge

Caine, Barbara, E. A. Grosz and Marie de Lepervanche (eds) (1988) *Crossing Boundaries: Feminisms and the critique of knowledges*, Sydney: Allen and Unwin

Cawelti, John G. (1976) *Adventure, Mystery, and Romance: Formula Stories as Art and Popular Culture*, Chicago and London: University of Chicago Press

Cixous, Hélène (1981) *Sorties* in Marks and de Courtivron (eds) *New French Feminisms*, pp. 90–8 [Fr 1975]

Cranny-Francis, Anne (1988) 'Sexual Politics and Political Repression in Bram Stoker's *Dracula*', in C. S. Bloom (ed.) *Nineteenth-Century Suspense: From Poe to Conan Doyle*, London: Macmillan, pp. 64–79

—— (1990a) 'De-fanging the vampire: S. M. Charnas' *The Vampire Tapestry* as subversive horror fiction' in Brian Docherty (ed.) *American Horror Fiction: From Brockden Brown to Stephen King*, London: Macmillan, pp. 155–75

—— (1990b) *Feminist Fiction: Feminist Revisions of Generic Fiction*, Cambridge: Polity Press; New York: St Martin's Press

—— (1991) 'Imaging the Writer: the Visual Semiotics of Book

Reviews', *Hecate: A Women's Interdisciplinary Journal* 17, 2, pp. 43–59

—— (1992) *Engendered Fiction: Analysing Gender in the Production and Reception of Texts*, Sydney: New South Wales University Press

—— (1994) *Popular Culture*, Geelong: Deakin University Press

Crary, Jonathan and Sanford Kwinter (eds) (1992) *Zone 6: Incorporations*, New York: Zone

de Lauretis, Teresa (1987) *Technologies of Gender: Essays on Theory, Film and Fiction*, Bloomington: Indiana University Press

—— (ed.) (1986) *Feminist Studies/Critical Studies*, Bloomington: Indiana University Press

Deleuze, Gilles and Félix Guattari (1983a) 'Rhizome' in *On the Line*, trans. John Johnston, New York: Semiotext(e)

—— (1983b) *Anti-Oedipus: Capitalism and Schizophrenia*, trans. R. Hurley, M. Steen and H. R. Lane, Minneapolis: University of Minnesota Press [Fr 1972]

Dempster, Elizabeth (1988) 'Women Writing the Body: Let's Watch a Little How She Dances' in Susan Sheridan (ed.) *Grafts: Feminist Cultural Criticism*, London: Verso, pp. 35–54

Dempster, Elizabeth, Sally Gardner, Anne Thompson and Jude Walton (eds) (1989) *Writings on Dance* vol. 4, *Making History*

Dery, Mark (ed.) (1993) *Flame Wars: The Discourse of Cyberculture*, special issue of *Southern Atlantic Quarterly* 92, 4

Dick, Philip K. (1972) *Do Androids Dream of Electric Sheep?*, London: Granada [1969]

Douglas, Mary (1966) *Purity and Danger*, London: Routledge and Kegan Paul

Fanon, Frantz (1967) *Black Skin White Masks*, New York: Grove Press

Featherstone, Cait (1991) 'Crib Colours Fade' in Susan Hawthorne and Renate Klein (eds) *Angels of Power and Other Reproductive Creations*, West Melbourne: Spinifex, pp. 84–6

Featherstone, Mike, Mike Hepworth and Bryan S. Turner (1991) *The Body: Social Process and Cultural Theory*, London: Sage

Feher, Michel, Ramona Naddaff and Nadia Tazi (1989a) *Zone 3:*

*Fragments for a History of the Human Body, Part I*, New York: Zone

—— (1989b) *Zone 4: Fragments for a History of the Human Body, Part II*, New York: Zone

—— (1989c) *Zone 5: Fragments for a History of the Human Body, Part III*, New York: Zone

Ferguson, Russell, Martha Gever, Trinh T. Minh-ha and Cornel West (eds) (1990) *Out There: Marginalization and Contemporary Cultures*, New York: The New Museum of Contemporary Art

Figes, Eva (1978) *Patriarchal Attitudes*, London: Virago

Finch, Lynette (1993) *The Classing Gaze: Sexuality, Class and Surveillance*, Sydney: Allen and Unwin

Foucault, Michel (1979) *Discipline and Punish: The Birth of the Prison*, New York: Vintage [Fr 1975]

—— (1981) *The History of Sexuality Volume One: An Introduction*, Harmondsworth: Pelican [Fr 1976]

—— (1986) *The Use of Pleasure: The History of Sexuality Volume Two*, London: Viking [Fr 1984]

—— (1988) *The Care of the Self: The History of Sexuality Volume Three*, London: Allen Lane [Fr 1984]

Frank, Lisa and Paul Smith (eds) (1993) *Madonnarama: Essays on Sex and Popular Culture*, Pennsylvania: Cleis Press

Friedman, Susan Stanford (1991) 'Creativity and the Childbirth Metaphor: Gender Difference in Literary Discourse' in Robyn R. Warhol and Diane Price Herndl (eds) *Feminisms: An Anthology of Literary Theory and Criticism*, New Brunswick, New Jersey: Rutgers University Press, pp. 371–96 [1987]

Frow, John (1990) 'Accounting for Tastes: Some Problems in Bourdieu's Sociology of Culture', *Cultural Studies* 1, pp. 59–73

Gaines, Jane and Charlotte Herzog (eds) *Fabrications: Costume and the Female Body*, New York and London: Routledge

Gallagher, Catherine and Thomas Laquer (1987) *The Making of the Modern Body: Sexuality and Society in the Nineteenth Century*, Berkeley: University of California Press

Gibson, William (1986) *Neuromancer*, London: Harper/Collins

Giddens, Anthony (1989) *Sociology*, Cambridge: Polity Press

Gilbert, Pam and Sandra Taylor (1991) *Fashioning the Feminine: Girls, Popular Culture and Schooling*, Sydney: Allen and Unwin

Gilbert, Sandra M. and Susan Gubar (1979) *The Madwoman in the Attic: The Woman Writer and the Nineteenth-Century Literary Imagination*, New Haven: Yale University Press

Gillard, Patricia (1986) *Girls and Television*, Sydney: N.S.W. Ministry of Education

Gilroy, Paul (1992) 'The end of anti-racism' in J. Donald and A. Rattansi (eds) *'Race', Culture and Difference*, London: Sage

Goldstein, Lawrence (ed.) (1991) *The Female Body: Figures, Styles, Speculations*, Ann Arbor: University of Michigan Press

Grosz, Elizabeth (1989) *Sexual Subversions: Three French Feminists*, Sydney: Allen and Unwin

—— (1990) 'Inscriptions and Body-maps: Representations and the Corporeal' in Terry Threadgold and Anne Cranny-Francis (eds) *Feminine/Masculine and Representation*, Sydney: Allen and Unwin, pp. 62–74

Gunew, Sneja (ed.) (1990) *Feminist Knowledge: Critique and Construct*, London and New York: Routledge

Hall, Stuart (1992) 'The Question of Cultural Identity' in Stuart Hall, David Held and Tony McGrew (eds) *Modernity and its Futures*, Cambridge: Polity Press, pp. 273–325

Haraway, Donna (1991) 'A Cyborg Manifesto: Science, Technology, and Socialist-Feminism in the Late Twentieth Century' in *Simians, Cyborgs and Women: The Reinvention of Nature*, New York: Routledge, pp. 149–81

Hardy, Thomas (1978) *Tess of the D'Urbervilles: A Pure Woman*, Harmondsworth: Penguin [1891]

Hekman, Susan J. (1990) *Gender and Knowledge: Elements of a Postmodern Feminism*, Cambridge: Polity Press

hooks, bell (1990) *Yearning: Race, Gender, and Cultural Politics*, Boston: South End Press

Idhe, Don (1990) *Technology and the Lifeworld: From Garden to Earth*, Bloomington: Indiana University Press

Irigaray, Luce (1985) *Speculum of the Other Woman*, trans. Gillian C. Gill, Ithaca, New York: Cornell University Press [Fr 1974]

—— (1985) *This Sex Which Is Not One*, trans. Catherine Porter and Carolyn Burke, Ithaca, New York: Cornell University Press [Fr 1977]

Jacobus, Mary, Evelyn Fox Keller and Sally Shuttleworth (eds) (1990) *Body/Politics: Women and the Discourses of Science*, New York and London: Routledge

Jardine, Alice (1987) *Gynesis: Configurations of Woman and Modernity*, Ithaca, New York: Cornell University Press

Jones, Ernest (1950) 'The Factory Town' in *A Chartist Anthology*, Moscow: Progress Press, pp. 141–5 [1847]

Kafka, Franz (1948) 'In the Penal Colony' in *The Penal Colony: Stories and Short Pieces*, trans. Willa and Edwin Muir, New York: Schocken [Ger 1919]

Kristeva, Julia (1982) *The Powers of Horror: An Essay on Abjection*, trans. Leon Roudiez, New York: Columbia University Press

Langton, Marcia (1993) *'Well, I Heard it on the Radio and I Saw it on the Television' . . . : An essay for the Australian Film Commission on the Politics and Aesthetics of Filmmaking by and about Aboriginal People and Things*, North Sydney: Australian Film Commission

Lawrence, D. H. (1960) *Lady Chatterley's Lover*, Harmondsworth: Penguin [1928]

Le Guin, Ursula (1981) *The Left Hand of Darkness*, London: Futura [1969]

Levy, Steven (1992) *Artificial Life: A Report from the Frontier Where Computers Meet Biology*, New York: Vintage

Lorde, Audre (1984) *Sister Outsider: Essays and Speeches*, Freedom, California: The Crossing Press

Lutz, Catherine A. and Jane L. Collins (1993) *Reading* National Geographic, Chicago and London: University of Chicago Press

Macarthur, Sally (1994) 'Keys to the Musical Body' in *Feminist Theory and Women's Studies in the 1990s*, Humanities Research Centre Summer School, Canberra, 2–5 February

McHoul, Alec and Wendy Grace (1993) *A Foucault Primer: Discourse, Power and the Subject*, Carlton: Melbourne University Press

McNay, Lois (1992) *Foucault and Feminism: Power, Gender and the Self*, Cambridge: Polity Press

Marks, Elaine and Isabelle de Courtivron (eds) (1981) *New French Feminisms: An Anthology*, Brighton, Sussex: Harvester

Martin, Emily (1987) *A Woman in the Body: A Cultural Analysis of Reproduction*, Boston: Beacon Press

MATRIX (ed.) (1984) *Making Space: Women and the Man-made Environment*, London and Sydney: Pluto Press

Mauss, Marcel (1992) 'Techniques of the Body', in Crary and Kwinter (eds) *Incorporations*, pp. 455–77 [1934]

Mead, Edward P. (1950) 'The Steam King' in *A Chartist Anthology*, Moscow: Progress Press, pp. 91–2 [1843]

Mercer, Kobena (1990) 'Black Hair/Style Politics' in Ferguson et al. (eds) *Out There*, pp. 247–64

Michie, Elsie (1992) 'From Simianized Irish to Oriental Despots: Heathcliff, Rochester and Racial Difference', *Novel: A Forum on Fiction* 25, 2, pp. 125–40

Minh-ha, Trinh (1991) 'Outside In Inside Out' in *When the Moon Waxes Red: Representation, Gender and Cultural Politics*, New York and London: Routledge, pp. 65–78

Moon, Brian (1992) *Literary Terms: A Practical Glossary*, Scarborough: Chalkface Press

Morgan, Sally (1987) *My Place*, Fremantle: Fremantle Arts Centre Press

Morris, William (1885) 'Attractive Labour', *Commonweal*, June Supplement, p. 49 col. 1– p. 50 col. 1

Morrison, Tony (ed.) (1992) *Race-ing Justice, En-gendering Power: Essays on Anita Hill, Clarence Thomas, and the Construction of Social Reality*, New York: Pantheon

Owens, Craig (1983) 'The Discourse of Others: Feminists and Postmodernism' in Hal Foster (ed.) *Postmodern Culture*, London and Sydney: Pluto Press, pp. 57–82

Pateman, Carole and Elizabeth Gross (eds) (1986) *Feminist Challenges: Social and Political Theory*, Sydney: Allen and Unwin

Penley, Constance and Andrew Ross (eds) (1991) *Technoculture*, Minneapolis: University of Minnesota Press

Piercy, Marge (1991) *Body of Glass*, London: Penguin

Poster, Mark (1992) 'RoboCop' in Crary and Kwinter (eds) *Incorporations*, pp. 436–40

Riviere, Joan (1986) 'Womanliness as a Masquerade' in Victor Burgin, James Donald and Cora Kaplan (eds) *Formations of Fantasy*, London and New York: Methuen, pp. 35–44 [1929]

Robinson, Hilary (ed.) (1987) *Visibly Female: Feminism and Art: An Anthology*, London: Camden Press

Rodriguez, Richard (1990) 'Complexion' in Ferguson et al. (eds) *Out There*, pp. 265–78

Russ, Joanna (1984) *How to Suppress Women's Writing*, London: Women's Press

Russell, Willy (1985) *Educating Rita*, London: Longman

Said, Edward (1978) *Orientalism*, London: Penguin

Sarsby, Jacqueline (1985) 'Sexual Segregation in the Pottery Industry', *Feminist Review* 21, pp. 67–93

Shelley, Mary (1982) *Frankenstein or The Modern Prometheus*, ed. Maurice Hindle, Harmondsworth: Penguin [1818]

Shepherd, John (1991) *Music as Social Text*, Cambridge: Polity Press

Shilling, Chris (1993) *The Body and Social Theory*, London: Sage

Sobchak, Vivian (1987) *Screening Space: The American Science Fiction Film*, 2nd edn, New York: Ungar

Spender, Dale (1989) *The Writing or the Sex? Or Why You Don't Have to Read Women's Writing to Know It's No Good*, New York: Pergamon

Steedman, Carolyn (1986) *Landscape for a Good Woman: A Story of Two Lives*, London: Virago Press

Stoker, Bram (1983) *Dracula*, Oxford: Oxford University Press [1897]

Stoller, Robert J. (1968) *Sex and Gender*, London: Hogarth Press

Tiptree, James, Jr (1975) 'The Women Men Don't See' in *Warm Worlds and Otherwise*, New York: Ballantine, pp. 131–64

Treichler, Paula (1990) 'Feminism, Medicine, and the Meaning of Childbirth' in Jacobus et al. (eds) *Body/Politics*, pp. 113–38

van Leeuwen, Theo (1988) 'Music and ideology: Notes towards a Sociosemiotics of Mass Media Music' in T. Threadgold (ed.) *Sydney Association for Studies in Society and Culture: Working Papers* 2, pp. 19–44

Vinge, Joan D. (1982) *Psion*, New York: Bantam
—— (1988) *Catspaw*, New York: Warner
Virilio, Paul (1991) *The Lost Dimension*, trans. Daniel Moshenberg, New York: Semiotext(e) [Fr 1984]
Walkerdine, Valerie (1989) *Counting Girls Out*, London: Virago Press
Walkerdine, Valerie and Helen Lucey (1989) *Democracy in the Kitchen: Regulating Mothers and Socialising Daughters*, London: Virago
Wells, H. G. (n.d.) *The Island of Doctor Moreau*, London: The Readers Library Publishing Co. [1896]
Willis, Paul (1980) *Learning to Labour: How Working Class Kids Get Working Class Jobs*, Aldershot, Hampshire: Gower
Winterson, Jeanette (1993) *Written on the Body*, London: Vintage
*Wired* (1993) 1, 3 (July–August)
Wittig, Monique (1981) 'One is Not Born a Woman', *Feminist Issues* vol. 1, no. 2

## Film and television

Burton, Tim (dir.) (1989) *Batman*, Warner
Cameron, James (dir.) (1984) *The Terminator*, Orion/Hemdale/Pacific Western
—— (dir.) (1986) *Aliens*, TCF/Brandywine
—— (dir.) (1990) *Terminator 2: Judgment Day*, Pacific Western
Campion, Jane (dir.) (1993) *The Piano*, Buena Vista
Fincher, David (dir.) (1992) *Alien*, Twentieth Century Fox/Brandywine
Fleischer, Richard (dir.) (1966) *Fantastic Voyage*, TCF
Gilbert, Lewis (dir.) (1983) *Educating Rita*, Columbia
Lyne, Adrian (dir.) (1987) *Fatal Attraction*, Paramount/Jaffe-Lansing
Murnau, F. W. (dir.) (1921) *Nosferatu*, Prana
Scott, Ridley (dir.) (1979) *Alien*, TCF/Brandywine
—— (dir.) (1982) *Blade Runner*, Warner/Ladd/Blade Runner Partnership

*Star Trek: the Next Generation* (1988-94) Paramount Pictures Corporation
Verhoeven, Paul (dir.) (1992) *Basic Instinct*, Carolco/Canal Plus
—— (dir.) (1987) *RoboCop*, Rank/Orion
Wilcox, Fred M. (dir.) (1956) *Forbidden Planet*, MGM

# Index


Aboriginal Australians, 48, 55, 64–5
aesthetics: as regulatory mechanism, 89; of racism, 51, 54–5, 56–7; of class, *see* taste
*Alien*, 15
Althusser, Louis, 10
anorexia, 3–4, 111–12
artists, 34, 36–8; female, 37–8

Barbin, Herculine, 29–30; *see also* Butler; Foucault
Belsey, Catherine, 11–12
Bernstein, Basil, 83, 86
Bhabha, Homi, x, 47, 50–5, 61, 62, 67
black: as primitive, 46; as political sign, 55–6, 62–3; *see also* colour
*Black Skin White Masks*, 53, 54
*Blade Runner*, 15, 88, 92
body: as evil, 4, 5, 22; as female, 36, 38, 41; as metaphor for creative product, 34–41; boundaries, 32, 86, 96–7, 98, 106; cyborg, 15–16, 91–105; defining the 'human', 88, 89, 92–4; generic, 23, 26; male, 14, 23, 24, 25; neutral, 26–7; normal, 1, 8–10; permeable, 95–7; postmodern, 12–14, 16–18, 36; techniques of the, 78–9, 86; transparent, 59; universal, 23, 24, 25; working-class men as, 76–7
Bordo, Susan, 3–4
Bourdieu, Pierre, 84–5
Butler, Judith, x, 27–33

Cameron, James, x, 15
Chartist poets, 89–90
childbirth, 9, 23, 25; as metaphor for creative production, 34–41; medicalisation of, 39–40; *see also* maternity; pregnancy; reproduction; reproductive technology
Christian theology, ix, 4, 22, 102
circumcision: female, 30; male, 30
Cixous, Hélène, 5–6, 36, 109
class, 66–87; as moral construct, 66, 68, 74; as sexual construct, 68–9; middle-class construction of, 66–77; cultures, 83; theorists of, 7–8
*Classing Gaze, The*, 68–9
colonialism, 45, 46–59
colour, skin, as political sign, 9–10, 53, 54, 55–6, 60, 62; *see also* black; whiteness
cyberspace, 16, 104; *see also Neuromancer*
cyborg, 2, 3, 15–16, 18, 91–105; *see also Blade Runner*; *Star Trek*; *Terminator 2*

dance, 108–9
Data, 15, 92, 94

Deleuze, Giles, 17–18; *see also* rhizome
Derrida, Jacques, 3, 13, 36, 50, 98
desire, 2, 16–18, 21, 102–5; class and, 67; colonialist, 47, 50, 52, 53; cybernetic, 102–5; heterosexual, 28; *see also* fantasies; stereotype
difference, 32, 50, 58, 60, 105; rejection of, 50–3, 83
*Distinction*, 84
Douglas, Mary, 32, 33, 42
Dracula, 72
drag, 31, 42
dualisms, 1; black/white, 57, 113; feminist critiques of, 4–7; human/alien, 113; human/machine, 113; instrument/receptacle, 5, 42; intellectual/physical, 35; male/female, 24, 113; man/woman, 5–6, 42; mental/manual, 7; mind/body, 1, 3–8, 17, 24, 34, 38–9, 42, 46, 74, 101, 113; masculine/feminine, 1, 15, 35; production/reproduction, 36–7, 38, 42; public/private, 6, 23–4; reality/representation, 2, 13–14

*Educating Rita*, 80–2
embodiment, *see* body
ethnic purity, 62–3
ethnicity, 59–63; defined, 61; theorists of, 7–8
experience, as political category, 1, 10–11, 33, 44, 46, 58–9, 81

family, 110–11
Fanon, Frantz, 52, 53, 54–5, 56, 67
fantasies: colonial, 48–9, 51, 54–5; class, 67–8
*Fashioning the Feminine*, 79–80
father, patriarchal, 35
femininity, new, 15, 109
feminist analysis: of the mind/body dualism, 4–7; of gender, 22–7
Figes, Eva, 4–5
Finch, Lynette, x, 68–9, 72–5
Foucault, Michel, 2–3, 18–21, 28, 29
*Frankenstein*, 35, 40–1, 88, 89, 91, 101
Freud, Sigmund, 10–11, 12, 16, 103

gender, 28, 29; as performance, 31–2; construction of, 79–80; in performance, 38–43
Gibson, William, 100, 101–2
Gilbert, Pam, 79–80
Gillard, Patricia, 80
Grosz, Elizabeth, 13, 16–17
Guattari, Felix, 17–18; *see also* rhizome

*habitus*, 84–5
hair, as cultural construct, 9, 56, 57–8, 61, 81
Hall, Stuart, 60, 61–2, 63
Haraway, Donna, 32, 98–99, 100–1, 102
Hardy, Thomas, 71, 72–3, 90
heterosexism, 29, 30, 31–2, 35
HIV/AIDS, 95, 96–7
hooks, bell, 44–5, 46, 47–8, 50, 53, 58, 62, 71–2

identity, 28–9
identity, politics of, 32–33, 43, 44–5, 53, 58, 60, 62–3, 66, 87, 98, 106
incest, 75
information superhighway, 94; *see also* technology
Irigaray, Luce, 12
IVF, *see* reproductive technology

King, Martin Luther, 7
Kristeva, Julia, 10, 17, 40

Lacan, Jacques, 11–12, 16–17, 103
*Landscape for a Good Woman*, 70, 83
Langton, Marcia, 48, 51
Lucey, Helen, 67–8, 70–1, 73, 79, 83

Madonna, 13–14, 48
masculinity, new, 15, 109–12
masquerade, femininity as, 27–8
maternity, 8–9, 23, 33–43, 67–8, 77; lesbian, 42; *see also* childbirth; reproduction
Mauss, Marcel, x, 67, 69, 77–9, 83–4
Mercer, Kobena, 56–8

middle class: fear, 67, 70–7; ideology of, 71, 77, 82, 86; violence of, 76; *see also* class
mind, positive valuations of, 1, 3, 7, 17, 24, 36, 46, 100, 102
mind/body dualism, 1, 3–8, 17, 24, 34, 38–9, 42, 46, 74, 101, 113; *see also* dualisms
Minh-ha, Trinh, 58, 59
Morgan, Sally, 64
Morris, William, 90–1
motherhood: belittled, 39; pathologised, 39–40; *see also* maternity; reproduction
music, 85–6, 107–8
*My Place*, 64–5

*National Geographic*, 46–7
network, 16, 17, 33, 98–9, 104–5
networking, 98–9
*Neuromancer*, 100, 101, 102
*Nosferatu*, 72

*Orientalism*, 51
other, 105; as colonialist construct, 51–9
otherness, 50, 63–5, 82

performer, body of the, 107–9
*Piano, The*, 75, 76
pregnancy, 8–9, 23, 25, 36, 38–9; pathologisation of, 39–40; *see also* childbirth
primitive, constructions of the, 46–7, 48
prostheses, 15–16, 93
*Purity and Danger*, 32

race, 44–59, 60; theorists of, 7–8
racist discourse, 54; *see also* stereotype
rape, as colonialist practice, 47
representation, 2, 13–14, 36; *see also* dualisms
reproduction: bodily, 23, 33–43; as second-order creativity, 36; *see also* childbirth
reproductive technology, 23, 40, 96; *see also* childbirth
resistance, 1, 10, 40, 59, 76–7
rhizome, 17–18, 102–5
Riviere, Joan, 27–8
Rodriguez, Richard, 56
Russell, Willy, 80–2

Said, Edward, 51, 53
Schwarzenegger, Arnold, 15, 110–11
Scott, Ridley, 15
sex: as 'neutral' category, 26–7; defined, 28, 30
sex/gender distinction, 25–7
sexuality: and class, 67, 70–2; and racism, 47, 49; as technology, 19–20, 33
Shelley, Mary, 35, 36, 88, 89; *see also* *Frankenstein*
Sherman, Cindy, 13–14
*Star Trek: The Next Generation*, 15, 92, 94
Steedman, Carolyn, 70–1, 83
stereotype: defining the, 50, 53–5; class, 67–8, 72, 73, 79, 85; race, 46–7, 48–59, 62, 63–4, 67
Stoker, Bram, 72
subjectivity, 1–2, 10–12, 17; postmodern interrogation of, 44–5

taste, class and, 83, 85; *see also* *Distinction*
Taylor, Sandra, 79–80
technology, ix, 2, 15–16, 34, 88–105, 106, 109–13; information, 63, 88, 89, 93, 98–102, 106; reproductive, 23, 40–1, 96; *see also* Chartist poets; cyborg; *Frankenstein*; Morris; Shelley; *Terminator 2*; Wells
*Terminator 2*, x, 15, 88, 92, 95–7, 109–12
*Tess of the D'Urbervilles*, 71, 72–3
Tiptree, James, 48–50

upper class, 72–3; *see also* class

Vinge, Joan, 103, 105, 113
violence, male: working-class, 74–5; middle-class, 74, 76

virtual reality, 101, 105; *see also* *Neuromancer*

Walkerdine, Valerie, 67–8, 70–1, 73, 79, 83
web, network as, 99
Wells, H. G., 91
wet-ware, 16, 99–102
whiteness, 45, 58, 59; *see also* colour
Winterson, Jeanette, x, xi
Wittig, Monique, 30, 31
women's magazines, 79–80, 86–7
working class: defined by middle class, 68–9, 73–7; men, 7, 73–6; women, 67–8, 70–1, 73, 75, 79, 80–2; *see also* class
workplace: gender and the, 24–5, 27; class and the, 83

X, Malcolm, 7, 58

Other Interpretations titles available from Melbourne University Press:

## After Mabo

*Interpreting indigenous traditions*

TIM ROWSE

Many non-Aboriginal Australians, sensitive to the fact that their nation came into existence through the conquest and dispossession of indigenous peoples, continue to seek ways of righting historical wrongs. A significant stage was reached in the High Court's so-called Mabo decision of June 1992, which recognised a 'native right in land'. Tim Rowse draws on history, political science, anthropology, cultural studies, ecology and archaeology to critique non-Aboriginal ways of perceiving Aboriginality. He focuses on the moral and legal traditions of settlers and indigenous peoples, their different attitudes towards the environment, the institutional heritage of 'Aboriginal welfare', tensions between indigenous cultures and indigenous politics, and the representation of Aboriginal identities by Aboriginal writers.

*'a stylish and shrewd book . . . should be read by all who try to follow Mabo' Barry Hill,* Age

## The Architecture of Babel

*Discourses of literature and science*

DAMIEN BRODERICK

Today the humanities seem painfully severed from the sciences. Writers, artists and ordinary thinking citizens cannot readily understand the sciences that have reshaped modern life. Scientists in turn find critical theory difficult and elusive. Drawing on recent semiotic and post-structural approaches to the text, Damien Broderick provides a critical introduction to recent efforts to construct an interdisciplinary analysis of the 'two cultures', literature and science. He finds literary theorists deficient in scientific rigour, and would like scientists to acquire the linguistic sophistication of humanists and their postmodern successors. Both literary theories and scientific practices, he concludes, are deeply implicated in social contexts.

*'an intriguing intellectual tour through exciting territory, much of which is at the cutting edge of literary and scientific philosophy' Robyn Arianrhod,* Age

## Cultural Materialism

ANDREW MILNER

For much of this century, idealist accounts sought to represent culture as 'pure' consciousness, while materialist accounts represented it as a secondary 'effect' of some other material reality. But from the 1970s new theoretical paradigms have attempted to establish the materiality of culture itself. This book is both an introduction and a contribution to cultural theory. It situates cultural materialism in relation to earlier paradigms such as literary humanism and Marxism, explains how it has been applied in such areas as cultural, media and literary studies, and explores the differences between British and French variants created by Raymond Williams, E. P. Thompson, Pierre Bourdieu and Michel Foucault.

*'The accomplishments of* Cultural Materialism *are substantial . . . Milner's work achieves considerably more than the definition of a literary theory' Noel Henricksen,* Australian Left Review

## Debating Derrida

NIALL LUCY

'There is nothing outside the text.' Possibly no single statement has caused such a storm in critical theory as this famous observation by the French philosopher, Jacques Derrida. While it is often misunderstood as meaning that nothing is real, *Debating Derrida* demonstrates that Derrida's philosophy does not lack political conviction.

Niall Lucy examines three key terms–text, writing and *différance*–as they are used in three famous debates: Derrida's disputes over speech-acts with John R. Searle, over discourse with Michel Foucault and over apartheid. Lucy also takes up the issue of Derrida's relationship to postmodernism. *Debating Derrida* decisively shows that instead of disagreeing with Derrida, we should rather be defending him.

## A Foucault Primer

*Discourse, power and the subject*

ALEC MCHOUL AND WENDY GRACE

The French historian and philosopher, Michel Foucault, has had a profound influence on scholars in the humanities and social sciences for the last three decades. This book is designed for those attempting to come to grips with Foucault's voluminous and complex writings. Instead of dealing with them chronologically, however, *A Foucault Primer* concentrates on some of their central concepts, primarily Foucault's rethinking of the categories of discourse, power and the subject (or subjectivity).

*'As an introductory account designed for the non-specialist reader, this book stands out' Paul Patton, University of Sydney*

## Framing and Interpretation

GALE MACLACHLAN AND IAN REID

The metaphor of 'framing' is commonly used by those who study socio-cultural texts, and appears to have developed independently in such various disciplines as linguistics, cultural studies, anthropology, psychology, literary criticism, artificial intelligence, aesthetics and the sociology of education. This book is the first to provide a cross-disciplinary exposition and systematic analysis of framing theory and its technical applications. Among the influential theorists of framing whose ideas are critically discussed, special attention is paid to Derrida, Goffman, Bateson, Tannen, Uspensky, Culler, Herrnstein Smith, Schapiro, Bernstein and Minsky.

*'This elegantly written and intriguing book provides an excellent introduction to framing theory' Ilana Snyder, Monash University*

## Framing Marginality

*Multicultural literary studies*

SNEJA GUNEW

What is the status of writings by minority ethnic groups in a country such as Australia, where the literature is in English and the dominant cultural traditions are Anglo-Celtic? How is our understanding of Australian literature affected by that heterogeneous collection of writings described as 'migrant' or 'multicultural'? Sneja Gunew draws on feminist, post-structuralist and post-colonial criticism to examine how non-Anglo-Celtic writings circulate in Australia, and how they are related to comparative multicultural studies, recent critiques of English studies as an imperial apparatus, and the deconstruction of 'universal' notions of culture by such scholars as Said, Bhabha, Spivak and Trinh.

## Literary Formations

*Post-colonialism, nationalism, globalism*

ANNE BREWSTER

*Literary Formations* provides a detailed examination of post-colonial literatures and literary theory. Writing from a feminist perspective, Brewster introduces the issue of gender into a field that has been widely dominated by questions of race and nationalism. She investigates the genre of Aboriginal women's autobiography and looks at the contrasting approaches to nationalism of two 'ethnic' women writers–Bharati Mukherjee in the USA and Ania Walwicz in Australia. Scrutinising the processes of neo-colonisation and the ways in which indigenous, diasporic and multicultural writing are reappropriated by the canon, *Literary Formations* is a valuable introduction to this influential area of critical thinking.

## Masculinities and Identities

DAVID BUCHBINDER

Why does masculinity find itself in crisis? This book traces some causes, as well as the developing interest in masculinity and the creation of men's studies, from their origins in feminist and gay political activist theory. David

Buchbinder examines the dynamics at work in various cultural constructions of masculinity, not all of which meet with approval in a patriarchal culture. The effects on men of patriarchal ideologies, phallocentrism and male sexuality (both heterosexual and homosexual) are among the issues discussed, while different strands of masculine discourse are identified and examined in a variety of texts ranging from opera to recent news stories.

*'a timely, sensible and sensitive book' David Gilbey,* Australian Book Review

## Metafictions?

*Reflexivity in contemporary texts*

WENCHE OMMUNDSEN

This book offers an introduction to a literary phenomenon that many find impenetrable or exasperating: 'metafiction', the fiction that is about writing fiction. *Metafictions?* argues that reflexivity is not marginal or derivative but a function central to all literary language. Neither is it a specifically contemporary or postmodern concern, although recent literary theory has increased awareness of the insights reflexivity has to offer on the nature of literary communication. Wenche Ommundsen explains the theoretical framework from which reflexivity is examined and extends the discussion to texts and literatures not generally alluded to in this tradition.

## Nuclear Criticism

*Ken Ruthven*

In the fallout from the obliteration of Hiroshima and Nagasaki was the seed of a new cultural phenomenon: a half-century of writings which attempt to evaluate the cultural consequences of nuclear technology. Ken Ruthven introduces a variety of analytical approaches to representations of nuclearism from official accounts of the first atomic test to recent nuclear controversies. The assumptions and practices of the self-styled, theoretically sophisticated Nuclear Criticism are examined and placed in context. *Nuclear Criticism* argues that a broadly based nuclear criticism should be a component of cultural studies in a post-Cold War period characterised by fewer nuclear weapons and more nuclear powers.

*'a most significant addition to an important and criminally under-regarded field' Frances Bonner,* Southern Review

## Postmodern Socialism

PETER BEILHARZ

Injustice, poverty, living and working conditions: the attempt to deal with these social questions arose from a nineteenth-century recognition of the complex problems created mainly in cities. At the same time socialism emerged from a romantic stream of Enlightenment concerned with nature and simplicity. Socialist arguments, now widely viewed as discredited, tackled these problems that ironically remain with us in these postmodern times. By juxtaposing postmodernity and socialism we can generate illuminating perspectives on the way we live *now. Postmodern Socialism* traces and criticises these perspectives.

> '*an intellectual* tour de force . . . *a vital contribution to the debate on* la fin de socialisme' *Manfred Steger,* Critical Sociology

## Reconstructing Theory

*Gadamer, Habermas, Luhmann*

EDITED BY DAVID ROBERTS

It seems that you cannot be taken seriously in critical thought these days if you are not *au fait* with the works of Foucault, Derrida and other French intellectuals. But there is an alternative tradition for those who find that deconstruction leads only to nihilism and despair.

*Reconstructing Theory* is an accessible and provocative introduction to the key thinkers of this alternative tradition. It investigates the contributions to social and cultural theory of Gadamer, Habermas and Luhmann, and analyses the influences of Jauss, Iser and Peter and Christa Bürger on literary theory. This book demonstrates that it may after all be possible not only to seek to explain and to criticise the world, but to humanise and even to change it.

## Theories of Desire

PATRICK FUERY

Lacan, Barthes, Derrida, Foucault, Kristeva, Cixous, Irigaray: these critical theorists are all linked by their analyses of desire. *Theories of Desire* looks not only at the role of desire in the works of these writers but also examines other major issues and themes of post-structuralism. Fuery considers the place of desire in psychoanalysis, philosophy, literary studies and feminism. He highlights the connections between desire and the critical analysis of subjectivity, language and culture. He investigates the institutionalisation of desire, the relationship between language, discourse and desire, and notes the problems of dealing with women's desire in phallocentric contexts.